I0658989

SIX WORDS YOU NEVER KNEW HAD SOMETHING TO DO WITH PIGS

To Gordon and Patricia Barber,
who instilled in me a passion for words,
a desire to learn foreign languages,
a love of history,
and an insatiable curiosity

Six Words You Never Knew Had Something to Do with Pigs

and Other Fascinating Facts About the Language from Canada's Word Lady

· KATHERINE BARBER ·

OXFORD
UNIVERSITY PRESS

OXFORD
UNIVERSITY PRESS

70 Wynford Drive, Don Mills, Ontario M3C 1J9
www.oup.com/ca

Oxford University Press is a department of the University of Oxford.
It furthers the University's objective of excellence in research, scholarship,
and education by publishing worldwide in

Oxford New York

Auckland Cape Town Dar es Salaam Hong Kong Karachi
Kuala Lumpur Madrid Melbourne Mexico City Nairobi
New Delhi Shanghai Taipei Toronto

With offices in

Argentina Austria Brazil Chile Czech Republic France Greece
Guatemala Hungary Italy Japan Poland Portugal Singapore
South Korea Switzerland Thailand Turkey Ukraine Vietnam

Oxford is a trade mark of Oxford University Press
in the UK and in certain other countries

Published in Canada
by Oxford University Press

Copyright © Oxford University Press Canada 2006

The moral rights of the author have been asserted

First published 2006

All rights reserved. No part of this publication may be reproduced,
stored in a retrieval system, or transmitted, in any form or by any means,
without the prior permission in writing of Oxford University Press,
or as expressly permitted by law, or under terms agreed with the appropriate
reprographics rights organization. Enquiries concerning reproduction
outside the scope of the above should be sent to the Rights Department,
Oxford University Press, at the address above.

You must not circulate this book in any other binding or cover
and you must impose this same condition on any acquirer.

Library and Archives Canada Cataloguing in Publication

Barber, Katherine, 1959-
Six words you never knew had something to do with pigs: and other
fascinating facts about the language from Canada's word lady / Katherine Barber.

ISBN-10: 0-19-542440-9
ISBN-13: 978-0-19-542440-9

1. English language--Etymology. I. Title.

PE1574.B37 2006 422 C2005-906534-6

Cover and text design: Brett J. Miller
Cover & text Illustrations: Ian Mitchell

2 3 4 - 09 08 07 06

This book is printed on environmentally responsible Rolland Enviro Cream.
Printed in Canada

CONTENTS

౮

PREFACE

&

Six Words you Never Knew had Something to Do With Pigs had its origins in a series of talks about word histories that I did as a regular segment on CBC Radio One's *Metro Morning* show in Toronto, and occasionally for other CBC stations. These talks always had a seasonal 'hook', and this is why this book is organized thematically, looking at the passing year in words. This organizing principle also allows for making much more interesting connections between words than an alphabetical listing.

I would be remiss if I failed to thank Helen Bagshaw, then a producer at CBC Radio, whose idea it was to have me do these regular segments. She made me the 'Word Lady' (although that moniker was bestowed on me by *Metro Morning*'s host Andy Barrie), and I am forever grateful to her. Others have played an important part in this book. My thanks to my colleagues in OUP Canada's Dictionary Department, Robert Pontisso and Heather Fitzgerald, who read the manuscript and made very useful suggestions. Jonathan Webb did his usual fine job of editing. John Simpson and Philip Durkin at the *Oxford English Dictionary* were always willing to answer my questions of the 'what was it called before?' type, as were Antoinette Healey and the staff at the *Dictionary of Old English* at the University of Toronto.

Bluff Your Way In Etymology:

A VERY BRIEF HISTORY OF THE ENGLISH LANGUAGE

ॐ

Before we start looking at the history of the language, you must learn the first rule of the successful bluffer: what we are talking about is *etymology*, not *entomology*. Entomology is the study of insects. This book is of no use to you on that subject.

THE ANGLO-SAXONS

English developed from Anglo-Saxon, the language brought to Britain—which was then inhabited by Celts—by Germanic tribes (the Angles, Saxons, and Jutes) from what is now northern Germany and Denmark in the 5th century AD. These invaders gave England its name, 'the land of the Angles', and provided the language with many common basic terms, for example 'man', 'woman', 'breed', 'work', 'eat', 'house', and 'shriek'. Anglo-Saxon is also known as Old English, and designates the English language up until about 1100.

In 597, a group of monks came as missionaries from Rome to strengthen Christianity in Britain. A few words came directly into English from Latin at this time, most of them connected with religion and learning, e.g. 'school', 'minister', 'pope', 'verse', 'candle', and 'mass'.

BLOODY VIKINGS or THE GREAT DANES

Starting in 792 and continuing for the next two centuries, Viking invaders came from Scandinavia and occupied a large part of eastern England and northern Britain. Many everyday words in modern English, such as 'leg', 'call', 'take', and 'dirt', come from their language, Old Norse, which is related to Anglo-Saxon. Many words starting with a *sk-* sound are from Old Norse, such as 'sky' and 'scream', the latter joining the language as a synonym for the already established Anglo-Saxon 'shriek'. Surprisingly, one of the most successful Old Norse usurpers of an Old English word is 'them'. This bumped out the Anglo-Saxon 'hem', which still survives however as ''em' in phrases like 'give it to 'em'. You may think (or be told) that you are guilty of sloppy pronunciation if you say this, but in fact you are just perpetuating the original form of the third person plural objective pronoun in English rather than using the Danish upstart.

STORMIN' NORMANS
In 1066, William the Conqueror of Normandy (also called William the Bastard, which epithet is apparently to be taken literally rather than figuratively) defeated the English King Harold at the Battle of Hastings, bringing the British Isles under Norman rule. The Normans spoke a dialect of French which was very much influenced by Germanic languages, since the Vikings had settled in Normandy at the same time they were invading England and Scotland. After the Norman Conquest, French became the language of the ruling classes. Many words in modern English that describe government and the legal system, as well as terms connected with cooking, came from French at this time, among them 'sovereign', 'court', 'govern', 'advise', and 'braise'. The Norman influence also resulted in English often having two words where one had done before, for instance using an Anglo-Saxon word to designate animals on the hoof ('calf', 'cow', 'sheep'), while using a French word to designate the animals as food ('veal', 'beef', 'mutton'). The Norman Conquest is responsible for English being a hybrid of Germanic and Romance languages, and created such drastic changes in the language that by 1100 Old English had evolved into something called Middle

English. The term 'Middle English' covers the period up to the time of Chaucer.

JUST HOW VULGAR WAS VULGAR LATIN?

Norman French, though it had some Germanic features, was nonetheless predominantly a Romance language, derived from Latin, or more particularly Vulgar (or popular) Latin. This was the everyday spoken language of the people, not the classical Latin that was used in literature. So, for instance, the popular Latin word for 'head' was a word meaning 'jug' (much as in English we use the word 'mug' for 'face'). This was *testa*, and explains why the modern French word for 'head' is *tête* rather than a derivative of the classical Latin word for head, *caput* (which has given us 'capital'). English inherited many Vulgar Latin words through French.

THE FRENCH SQUISHING SYNDROME

As Vulgar Latin had evolved in Gaul into something called Gallo-Romance, a very common phenomenon was the reduction of multisyllable Latin words into shorter Old French words, usually by the removal of a few consonants in the middle (what I like to call the 'French Squishing Syndrome'). Whether this was due to slurry French speech habits induced by overindulgence in wine is lost in the mists of time. But, for instance, Latin *neptis* ended up as *niece* in Old French, *hospitale* became *ostel*, and *securus* became *sur*. By the time the Norman French came to England, this is what Latin had been reduced to in the former Gaul, and these were the forms that entered English, rather than the original Latin words. This is one of the reasons why we have many doublets in English.

WHAT IS A DOUBLET? IS IT A JACKET WORN WITH TIGHTS?

A doublet is one of two or more words derived ultimately from the same source, often because one came into the language directly and the other took a more circuitous route. English has many doublets from Latin sources. Usually the earlier word came from Norman French and the later one came from central French (either of which would have suffered the French Squishing Syndrome) or directly (unsquished) from Latin. Occasionally we have three words, or a triplet, from the same source, as in 'cattle' (from Norman French), 'chattel' (from central French), and 'capital', all derived from the Latin *capitalis* meaning 'of the head'. Another example is 'hostel' (from Old French), 'hospital' (from Latin), and 'hotel' (from modern French), all derived from the Latin *hospitale*.

MIND YOUR G's AND W's

Another source of doublets was the difference in the French spoken by the Norman invaders of England and the central French, who had a stronger influence on English a few centuries later. After the fall of the Roman Empire, the Franks—a Germanic people from the lower Rhinelands—invaded Gaul, establishing themselves in Northern France by the early 500s. Their Germanic language, Frankish, had lots of words beginning with *w*, like *werra* (war), and *werenta* (surety). But the Gauls living in central France, who were speaking the Latin-derived Gallo-Romance, had no initial *w* sound, so to make these Germanic words easier to say, they put a *g* in front, giving *guerra* and *guarantie*. But in areas in France of heavy Germanic population, such as Normandy (which had been invaded by Vikings) and the North, where the dialect was more heavily influenced by Germanic, the initial *w* managed to survive in words like 'warrant', 'ward', and 'war', whereas in central France these got changed to *garant*, *garde*, and *guerre*. But it wasn't the initial *g*-speaking central French who invaded England in 1066. It was of course the Normans, who brought Old Northern French (initial *w*'s and all) with them. The English, being Germanic speakers, of course had no difficulty with these *w*-words. Only later was there a stronger influence from central

French, which brought in the *g-* doublets for some words, hence 'warranty' (earliest recorded use in 1338) and 'guarantee' (1679), 'warden' (1225) and 'guardian' (1477). Of course, central French was the language of Paris and came to dominate all other dialects. That is why the *w-* variants no longer exist in modern French. But who knows what would have happened had William the Conqueror (whose very name demonstrates this linguistic tendency, since it is *Guillaume* in French) stayed home and turned his conquering ways towards Paris instead of Hastings?

ARABIC

From the 8th century to the 15th, the Iberian peninsula was to a lesser or greater degree under the control of Arabic speakers. A great Arabic culture flourished there, and many words relating to mathematics and astronomy, in particular, entered European languages from Arabic. In addition, during the Christian military expeditions to the Middle East in the 12th and 13th centuries, English Crusaders came into contact with the Arab world and brought some Arabic words back to England. These words tended to relate to Islam, to Arab society and culture, and to learning, or to designate plants from warmer climes. Among the words with Arabic origins in English are 'syrup', 'orange', 'alcohol', 'assassin', 'algebra', and 'alchemy'. Words starting in *al-* commonly come from Arabic, since *al-* was the definite article.

THE GREAT VOWEL SHIFT

Unlike 'French Squishing Syndrome', 'Great Vowel Shift' is an actual term used by linguists. Please feel free to use it at parties to impress people, but make sure you get the name right and don't call it the great bowel movement. The Great Vowel Shift was a change in English pronunciation that happened between about 1400 and about 1600. Before that time, the relationship between the pronunciation and spelling of vowels in English was similar to that in modern European languages. So 'fine' was pronounced FEEN and 'house' was pronounced HOOZ. For some reason, starting in about Chaucer's time, these pronunciations all shifted to their current ones, although the spelling remained unchanged (one of the many reasons why English spelling is so difficult). In a sort of domino effect, many other stressed vowels moved as well to fill the gaps thus created. So with the vowel in 'fine' moving away from FEEN, the vowel in 'see' (previously pronounced SAY) moved into that gap, and then the vowel in 'fame' (previously pronounced FAMM) moved into the spot vacated by 'see'. It was like a Virginia reel going on in people's mouths (no wonder the vowels were stressed).

SIR WALTER SCOTT

Many English words that existed in the Middle Ages died out for several centuries until revived by Sir Walter Scott (1771–1832). He wrote historical novels, and there was a great deal of interest in the Middle Ages in the 19th century. To add some local colour to his books he used a lot of archaic words. He was a huge bestseller, the Daniclle Steele or Stephen King of pre-Victorian England. Everyone read Sir Walter Scott. Because he had so many readers, many of the words that he revived stuck in the language, and he really is a phenomenon in the history of English.

THE RENAISSANCE BUSYBODIES

Many words of Latin origin came into English through French (having suffered the dread squishing syndrome) after the Norman Conquest. Latin was, of course, the language of learning throughout the Middle Ages, so some words also entered English directly from Latin then, such as 'graduate'. But the Renaissance of the 15th and 16th centuries brought new interest in Classical learning and an influx of words directly from Latin and Greek, such as 'physics', 'architecture', 'compute', 'radius', and 'academy'. At the same time, people started looking at the history of English words and insisting that their spelling reflect their Latin (or Greek) etymology if they had one, rather than just representing the pronunciation. Letters that had been lost in the Great French Squishing Syndrome before words even came into English were suddenly reintroduced to the spelling, though they remained unpronounced. As if the Great Vowel Shift going on at the same time wasn't already enough to create havoc for children learning to spell, to this interference we owe a lot of our silent letters, like the *b* in 'debt', the *s* in 'island', the *h* in 'thyme', and the ridiculous *p* in 'ptarmigan'. Thank goodness they didn't do more, or we would have to spell 'dainty' as 'daignty' and 'almond' as 'almognd'.

SAMUEL JOHNSON

Little knowing what he was letting himself in for, the man of letters Samuel Johnson (1709–84) signed a contract in 1746 to write a dictionary of the English language. He started out thinking that he could thus guard the purity of the language, but in the course of his work realized that this was impossible. In his preface, he admitted that his task was not to form the language but to record it, and that no nation has 'preserved their words and phrases from mutability.' Published in 1755, the dictionary was the first to use quotations from literature to illustrate the definitions. Johnson's dictionary was very successful, and helped to standardize English spelling.

BOTH A BORROWER AND A LENDER BE

With expanded English trade, travel, exploration, and colonization, starting in the 16th century, English spread to many parts of the world, and in turn it was influenced by the native languages of these lands. English speakers continue to this day to borrow abundantly from a wide variety of other languages. Words like 'sauna', 'futon', 'tea', 'tattoo', 'chipmunk', and 'toboggan' all come from languages that are neither Romance nor Germanic. At the same time, other languages have been borrowing from English as it has become a worldwide prestige language, often also creating trendy English-sounding words that don't actually exist in English. For instance, German-speakers call a cellphone a '*Handy*', and the French call a cut and blowdry '*un brushing*'.

WHY USE ONE WORD WHEN FIVE WILL DO?

As a result of absorbing words from all of these sources, English often has many synonyms from different languages to express the same idea, such as 'fear' (from Old English), 'terror' (from French in the 15th century), 'alarm' (from Italian), 'anxiety' and 'trepidation' (from Latin in the 16th and 17th centuries respectively), and 'angst' (from German in the 20th century).

THE 'YOU CAN'T USE NOUNS AS VERBS' MYTH

Many self-described 'language lovers' inveigh against what they call 'using nouns as verbs'. Without exception, they give the word 'impact' as the most nefarious example of what they perceive as this dreadful modern tendency. I am quite at a loss to explain why their hatred for the verb 'impact' has been expanded to a blanket condemnation of what is, and always has been, a common and very useful practice in English. Do these people never *mail* letters, *book* hotel rooms, *butter* toast, or take planes that *land*? Please, if you ever find yourself saying this, get over it. There is no such 'rule' in English. If we eliminated from our vocabulary all words that started out as one part of speech but became another, we would be quite literally at a loss for words.

NOWT SO QUEER AS FOLK ETYMOLOGIES

People love word histories and want them to be as complicated and surprising as possible Presumably that's why you're reading this book! What people hate is when a stodgy dictionary says 'origin unknown'. 'How can that be?' the word lovers think. 'There must be a really good story behind this one.' So they make one up. The more far-fetched, the better. These are the dreaded folk etymologies. They are not a new invention; English speakers have been inventing folk etymologies for centuries, witness the word 'sirloin' (see EATING OUT ON CANADA DAY, page 61). With the Internet, they now get circulated even more quickly and widely.

There are some sure signs that a purported word history is actually a folk etymology. Often the explanation states that the word is derived from an acronym, such as 'Fornication Under the Consent of the King' or 'For Unlawful Carnal Knowledge', and involves some implausible story (see also ALCOHOL in HAPPY NEW YEAR!, page 171). A painful pun or play on words can be involved. Frequently an eponymous origin is ascribed to the word, for instance that the word 'doozy' is derived from a car called a Duesenberg. It is very easy to check out many folk etymologies, and I implore you to do this the next time you get an entertaining word history forwarded to you in your email. Start with a respectable dictionary that includes etymologies. If it says 'origin uncertain', you can be sure that the lexicographers have looked into all the possible suggestions and found none of them compelling (so please don't write to us to say that you know for a fact that 'posh' comes from 'port outward starboard home'). If you want more information, you can consult the *Oxford English Dictionary* (OED) at most libraries, and find out when the word (or meaning of the word) entered the language. Often the first date will be earlier or much later than the purported source of the word given in the folk etymology. There are more than enough fascinating and true word histories; we don't need to make them up!

SPRING

Down on the Farm

&

Spring is a busy time on the farm, what with cows calving, mares foaling, and sows, well, pigging. Many common English words started out with a now totally forgotten connection to domestic livestock.

Cows

PECULIAR

'Peculiar' comes from the Latin word *pecu* meaning cattle. From this arose a derivative, *peculium*, meaning 'property', since cattle were private property. The adjective related to this was *peculiaris*, which meant 'relating to private property'. So 'peculiar' came to designate things that were a person's private property, something that belonged to you and no one else. You could say of a politician that he 'had not so much advanced the common wealth as his own private things and peculiar estate'. (That's a quotation from 1548, which just goes to show that some things never change!) From designating material things such as possessions, 'peculiar' soon came to be applied also to more abstract qualities and characteristics that were unique or 'peculiar' to one person or group. And since anything that distinguishes one person from the rest of humanity usually becomes stigmatized as strangeness, 'peculiar' eventually came to mean downright odd.

Incidentally, another word that came from this Latin word for cattle is 'pecuniary', because cattle signified wealth and money.

FELLOW

'Fellow' also comes from a word that meant cattle, and by extension money, but this time in Old Norse: the word *fé*. It had a derivative *félagi*, which was a person who laid down money in a joint enterprise, a partner or team member. Gradually the meaning became weakened to apply to anyone who was loosely associated with another, as in 'fellow traveller'. By the late 1400s 'fellow' was being used simply as a synonym for 'man' or 'guy'.

BUGLE

'Bugle' comes from the Latin *buculus,* which was a diminutive of the Romans' word for 'ox'. Originally 'bugle' in English meant a wild ox or even a buffalo. But wild ox horns made perfect hunting horns, so 'bugle' came to mean this simple type of horn. When the Hanoverian light infantry adopted copper hunting horns as their signalling instrument in about 1750, the name for the older hunting horn stuck.

BUCOLIC

'Bucolic' is also derived from this same Latin word for ox; a *bucolicus* was a herdsman. So 'bucolic' started out meaning literally 'related to herdsmen', but by the 1800s it was being used in the current sense of 'pertaining to country life'.

BULIMIA

The word 'bulimia', or at least variants of it, has been around a surprisingly long time. Even in 1398 people were talking about 'bolismus', which they defined as 'an immoderate or unmeasurable as it were an houndes appetyte'. It comes from two Greek words, *bous* meaning 'ox' and *limos* meaning 'hunger'. So, I guess, for a Greek you weren't hungry as a wolf but hungry as an ox. A late Victorian lexicon of medical terms defined 'bulimy' (as it was then spelled) as 'a morbid hunger, chiefly occurring in idiots and maniacs'. A bit harsh. It was not until the mid-1970s that bulimia, or binge eating, was identified as an eating disorder.

Pigs

PORCELAIN

'Porcelain' comes from the French word *porcelaine*, which in the Middle Ages was the word for a cowrie shell, one of those oval-shaped seashells with a very shiny surface. If you think of the shiny, ceramic-like quality of a cowrie shell, you can see why *porcelaine* came to be applied to bone china. But the interesting thing is how a cowrie shell came to be called *porcelaine*. The French had got it from Italian *porcellana*, which was a derivative of *porcella*, meaning a female pig. Although nothing has been proven, some dictionaries will tell you that the connection between pigs and cowries is that a cowrie looks like the back of a pig, while others will tell you that, if you flip a cowrie over, it looks like a pig's vulva. I don't know what sort of mind can think of that when looking at a seashell, but that's the story.

SCREW

'Screw' comes from the Old French *escroue*, which has become the Modern French word *écrou*, for 'nut', not the nut you eat but the nut you screw onto a bolt. *Escroue* came from Latin *scrofa,* which meant 'sow'. Again, we're looking at female pigs. I never realized that people spent this much time looking at female pigs. Anyway, no one really knows what the connection is, but one can only speculate that the curly tail was what people had in mind when they made this connection between sows and screws.

SOIL

This is 'soil' in the sense of making dirty or staining. In modern French, the verb meaning 'to make dirty' is *souiller*. In Old French this was *soillier*, and this is what came into English. The French word was a corruption of a popular Latin verb, *suculare*, which comes from *suculus* meaning 'a little pig'. And the earliest use of this word 'soil' as a noun in English meant literally 'a muddy place used by a wild boar for wallowing in'. So that's how we ended up with 'soil' meaning 'make dirty'. The other soil comes from the Latin word *solum* meaning 'ground'. So even though you might think they were related because they both have this connection with dirt, they're from two totally different sources.

PORPOISE

In Old French, *porpeis* was a squished-down corruption of the Latin *porcus piscis*, which meant literally 'pig fish'. Goodness knows why we spell it as we do, since this word has had at least forty spellings since it entered English in about 1300, and we could have ended up with just about any of them. Samuel Johnson, however, used the spellings 'porpoise' or 'porpus' in his dictionary, which probably helped the former win out. But it's really quite a ridiculous spelling when you look at it

ROOT

The verb 'root' in the sense of rummaging around, which was written 'wroot' until about 1600, was originally used only of pigs grubbing around looking for food with their snouts. This goes back to Anglo-Saxon times, but it wasn't until the 19th century that 'root around' started to be used of human beings.

SWAIN

Though 'swain' now survives only as a jocular word for a lover (and as an element meaning 'man' in the words 'boatswain' and 'coxswain'), it started out among the pigs. In Anglo-Saxon times, *swán* was the word for a swineherd. The word was obviously upwardly mobile, however, because it made its way from someone who tended to swine, to a knight's attendant, a male servant, a farm labourer, and a shepherd. The connection with lovers came about because, in the pastoral poetry of the 17th and 18th centuries, the young lover was often a shepherd.

Horses

WALLOP

The ultimate source for the word 'wallop' was a phrase in the language of the Franks, *wala hlaupan*, which meant 'run well' or 'run fast'. This Frankish phrase was related to the same Germanic words that gave English 'well' and 'leap'. When the Franks invaded France, they brought *wala hlaupan* with them, and in Northern French this became *waloper,* which meant, not 'wallop' as we know it today, but 'gallop'. It was of course the Normans, speakers of Northern French, who invaded England, where they became the landowners, the people who had the wealth to maintain horses for riding. With their arrival, French words started to usurp Anglo-Saxon words for equestrian matters. And *walop* was one of these words. So from about Chaucer's time to Henry VIII's time, horses went walloping down the roads in England. But meanwhile, back at the horse ranch in central France, the people had a hard time pronouncing these Frankish words beginning in *w* and stuck a *g* in there to make it easier, so *waloper* became *galoper* in Parisian French. And for some reason, in the 1500s the English decided they didn't want to use 'wallop' anymore and borrowed this French word instead. So 'gallop' ousted 'wallop' in the horse-riding sense, but 'wallop' started to take on other meanings. The first was 'boil noisily', what we would call a rolling boil, presumably in imitation of the sound made by horses' hooves. Then it meant to make violent, heavy, noisy movements. It wasn't until the early 1800s that it meant 'beat or strike', as it does today.

CANTER

'Canter' was shortened from the compound noun 'Canterbury pace' or 'Canterbury gallop' in the 1700s. The longer form had been around for about 100 years by then, and the explanation of it is that a 'Canterbury pace' was the speed at which the pilgrims proceeded on horseback to the shrine of St Thomas à Becket in Canterbury.

RANDOM

This word was 'randon' in about 1300 when we borrowed it from French. It came from a verb that meant 'to gallop', and even today in modern French there is a word *randonnée* which can mean a horseback (or bicycle) ride. So *randon* came into English as a noun meaning 'impetuosity' or 'great speed in riding': if you said someone rode their horse 'in a randon', it meant that they were riding at full speed and without much care. By Shakespeare's time, 250 years later, 'randon' had become 'random' and 'at random' meant what it does today—haphazardly, without a particular aim or purpose. It wasn't until the 1650s that an adjective developed, meaning 'done without conscious choice'. There is a wonderful quote from 1655: 'In vain do staid heads make serious comments on light men's random expressions.'

CURTAIL

The word 'curtail' was originally 'curtal' (pronounced CURTLE). We borrowed it from the French *courtault* in the early 1500s, to mean a horse whose tail has been docked, and also as a verb to mean the action of docking a horse's tail. Now, although the meaning of the word had this connection with horses' tails, the word itself was in no way related to the word 'tail' in English. *Courtault* (which has survived in the family name Courtauld, as in the Courtauld Collection of art in England), was simply a derivative of the French word *court* meaning 'short'. But, not surprisingly, people began to associate the second syllable of 'curtal' with the word 'tail', and a variant 'curtail' (still pronounced with the stress on the first sylla-ble, CURtail) sprang up very quickly. The other thing that happened almost immediately was that the verb 'curtal' or 'curtail' started to be used figuratively to mean 'cut short'. By the 1700s, 'curtail' defeated the 'curtal' variant, though it wasn't pronounced curTAIL till the 1800s. And here's a quotation from 1781 that I think we can all agree with: 'Greatly to curtaill salaries is a false economy.'

BIDET

There was an Old French word in the 1300s, *bider*, which meant 'to trot'. This gave rise in about the 1500s to a noun *bidet*, which meant a donkey or a small pony. The word also had this sense in English from the 1600s to the 1800s. In 1630, Ben Jonson could say, 'I will return to myself, mount my bidet, in a dance, and curvet upon my curtal'! The word was transferred to the name of the bathroom fixture in the 1750s, again in France, the idea being that one sat astride it like a horse. The English were obviously fas-cinated by this French invention, because they started talking about it a mere fifteen years later.

GIVE ME A BREAK!

ॐ

It's spring. Well, it should be spring, but in many parts of Canada, it's still the tail end of winter and people are eager to get away from the unending snow. March Break (itself a Canadian term) gives us the perfect opportunity to get away from it all by exploring some familiar travel-related words.

TRAVEL

The word 'travel' itself comes from a Latin word which means 'an instrument of torture'. The Latin word was *trepalium*, from *tres* meaning 'three' and *palus,* which was a stake or pointed stick. It probably doesn't bear thinking about how they used these three-pointed sticks as an instrument of torture. The French took this Latin word and squished it down a bit into *travail*, which, of course, is still the French word for work (which many people think of as torture, I'm sure). The English borrowed it from the French in the Middle Ages; the English word was pronounced traVALE, and it too meant 'work'. It could also mean both 'be in labour'—which fits with the idea of torture—as well as, interestingly, 'going on a trip', probably because that was such an arduous undertaking back then. Eventually, 'travail' dropped out of the language, and the word came to be pronounced TRAVVLE, and spelled 'travel'.

The dramatic changes that 'travel' and many, many other English words have undergone over the years illustrate why it's so illogical to argue about any word—'Well, originally in Latin it meant such and such'—because words evolve continually and it doesn't matter what they originally meant. What matters is what they mean now.

JOURNEY

'Journey' comes to us from the French *journée*, which means 'a day'. More specifically, in the Middle Ages, a journey was a day spent travelling, or the distance typically travelled in a day, which, it must be said, in the Middle Ages was only about twenty miles. But by the 1300s, a 'journey' had come to mean any expedition. Nowadays 'journey' is used very little in the literal sense, being reserved for more figurative uses.

'Journey' could also mean the work completed in a day, and this accounts for the word 'journeyman', which entered the language in the late 1400s.

TICKET

'Ticket' came into the language via Irish and Scottish in the 1500s, from a French word *étiquet* or *estiquet*. The Old French verb *estiquer* meant 'to stick', and an *estiquet* was a sort of written notice stuck up in a public place, usually a bailiff's notice affixed to people's doors to tell them their possessions were about to be removed. In English, the word got shortened to 'ticket' and meant a public notice, either one posted in a public place or a warrant or licence asserting someone's right to do something. From this sense, it was just a short step to the piece of paper entitling the holder to some service or privilege, such as boarding a plane.

FARE

The verb 'fare' started out in Old English as the word meaning 'travel'. It is related to the German word for 'go', *fahren*. So when you say 'farewell' to someone, you're actually saying, 'Have a good trip!' The verb 'fare' is now used only in the phrases 'fare well' or 'fare badly', meaning to have much or little success. The noun 'fare' started out meaning a trip, and it could also mean the equipment taken on a trip or a group of people setting out on a trip. But by the 1400s it meant the price you paid to travel somewhere.

When you hear taxi drivers talking about the people they pick up as their 'fares', you probably think it is some 20th-century slang innovation, but this use of 'fare' has actually been around since the mid-1500s.

TARMAC
This is a combination of 'tar' plus 'macadam', macadam being the type of road construction developed by the Scottish surveyor of the early 1800s, John McAdam. Macadam consisted of two layers of broken stone, and it revolutionized the road-building industry and hence communications in the 19th century. The tar version, which incorporated iron slag, tar, and creosote, saw the light of day in 1903, just in time to be used for airport runways.

PILOT
'Pilot' came into English from French in the early 1500s. It replaced a word that the English had been quite happy with until then, which was 'steersman'. We don't really know why they decided they needed a nifty new French word, but they did. The French had got it from medieval Latin, which in turn had derived it from the Greek *pēdota*, which came from *pedon*, meaning 'oar or rudder'. Since there were no aircraft, 'pilot' was originally confined to people steering boats, but in the 19th century we start to see pilots in hot-air balloons, and then, just two years after the Wright brothers made their first flight in 1905, 'pilot' was being used of fliers, although for a couple of decades people seemed to feel the need to say 'air pilot' to make the distinction.

STEWARD, STEWARDESS
'Steward' (and its Scottish variant 'stewart', which survives in family and given names) is a very old word that goes back to two old English elements, *stig*, which seems to have meant 'a house or part of a house', and *weard*, which meant 'keeper'. This word is related

to the word that has given us 'sty', but it doesn't seem to be true that originally a steward (or a Stewart, lest anyone by that name should be reading this) was a keeper of pigsties! In Anglo-Saxon times, a steward was the person in charge of a household. By 1450 the word was also being used to mean a ship's officer who supervised the serving of meals and attended to the passengers. Naturally, with the invention of passenger aircraft, this job was extended to aviation.

'Stewardess' arose in the 1600s to mean a female performing the duties of a steward (usually such uses were figurative). In the 1800s it was used to mean a woman who waited on female passengers on a ship, but only came into its own from about 1930. It seems to have been first used by United Airlines, in 1931. Of course, the word has now lost favour and been replaced by the gender-neutral 'flight attendant', which has actually been around since 1947, but became much more frequent from the mid-70s on.

LIMOUSINE
This comes from the name of one of the old provinces of France, Limousin, which is in the southwest, centred around Limoges. The shepherds in Limousin wore a kind of cloak with a big hood, which came to be called a *limousine*. Then, in the early 1900s, a kind of luxurious car was developed that had a seat for a chauffeur in the front which was separated from the back by a partition. The driver was under his own separate roof that I guess looked a little like a hood. Since this recalled the Limousin shepherd's cloak, the car was called a limousine.

TAXI
In the late 19th century the Germans developed a device that recorded the distance a vehicle travelled and the time it took to do so, so that a fare could be calculated. This they called a *Taxameter*, from the Latin *taxa* meaning 'tax' and *meter* meaning 'a measuring device'. So we could have ended up taking 'taxas' rather than

'taxis'. The taxameter caught on quickly in German cities in the 1890s, and from there spread to France. The English didn't get interested until about 1898, and there was strong resistance from the drivers of hansom cabs. By 1907, as motorized cabs became more common, it was decided that they should be fitted with the device, which was by then called a 'taximeter', based on the French form of the word. The fare was set at eightpence per mile or ten minutes. Tensions were high between the drivers of horse-drawn and horseless cabs: we have a report from 1907 of a horse-cab driver charged with assaulting a 'taximeter cab' driver. 'Taximeter cab' was a bit of a mouthful, so right away in 1907 'taxi-cab' was being used as a short form. Indeed, it seems that taxis were *the* hot topic for London journalists, who competed to think up names for this new invention. So 'taxi' also dates from 1907, was well established by 1908, and was used in a play by Shaw in 1911. I guess taxis made their way slowly through London traffic (some things never change), so when pilots needed a word shortly after that to mean 'travelling slowly along the tarmac', they invented the verb 'taxi'. This was in 1911.

CAB

The amazing thing about the word 'cab' is that it comes ultimately from the Latin word for 'goat'. 'Cab' started out in the 1820s as a shortened form of 'cabriolet', which was a light, two-wheeled, hooded one-horse carriage. 'Cab' quickly came to apply to any carriage that was for public hire. We borrowed 'cabriolet' in the mid-1700s from the French, who had given the carriage this name because it bounced up and down a lot, and a *cabriole* in French is a kind of springy jump. Before it meant 'springy jump', however, *cabriole* meant a young goat (goats, after all, are renowned for jumping about lightly), derived from the Latin word *capra* for 'goat'. So just think, we could have ended up talking about taximeter-cabriolets instead of taxicabs!

HACK

'Hack' is a shortened form (dating from the late 1600s) of 'hackney carriage', which is what taxis are still officially called in Britain. Indeed, I have a photo I took of a taxi outside Swindon railway station in Wiltshire about twenty years ago. It had a huge licence plate saying 'Hackney carriage licensed to carry 5 passengers'. (I may be the only tourist who takes pictures of taxi licence plates!) A 'hackney' was originally, back in the 1300s, a medium-sized horse for ordinary riding, not a war horse, hunting horse, or farm horse. They were called 'hackneys' after the place called Hackney, now part of East London, which was used for pasturing horses in the Middle Ages. Since this kind of horse was frequently hired out (it being very expensive to own a horse, they had a kind of medieval Hertz-Rent-a-Horse), 'hackney' soon came to mean a horse kept for hire. I guess you would get unlimited mileage on your rental horse, but we don't know if you had to fill it up with a bale of hay before returning it to the rental place! It was a logical extension to use 'hackney' also for a hired horse-drawn carriage.

Knowing this history, two other uses of 'hackney' and 'hack' make perfect sense. A hackneyed expression is one that has been used over and over again like a 'rental horse' or a carriage for hire. A 'hack writer' was originally one who hired himself out to do any kind of writing required of him. Nowadays 'hack' is a jocular, somewhat disparaging, name for a journalist.

DISPATCHER

'Dispatch' seems to have come into English from Italian or Spanish in the early 1500s to mean the sending of an official message. At this time the English court had a lot of dealings with Spain (since Henry VIII was at the time married to Catherine of Aragon) and with the Papal Court (possibly because of Henry VIII's attempts to be unmarried from Catherine of Aragon!), and 'dispatch' is a word much used in diplomatic circles. It competed for a while with a word meaning the same thing derived from French, 'depeach' (*dépêcher* in French means 'to hurry along'). For whatever reason, 'dispatch' won out; otherwise we'd have to talk about taximeter-cabriolet depeachers!

LUGGAGE

'Luggage' obviously comes from 'lug', but lug has not always meant 'to carry something heavy'. In fact, when it appeared in English in the 1300s, probably from a Scandinavian source, it meant to pull a person's hair or tug at their ear. But it quickly came to have its present meaning. So by Shakespeare's time, 'luggage' meant anything that was lugged about, and specifically one's bags when travelling.

HOTEL, HOSTEL

Both 'hotel' and 'hostel' can be traced to the Latin word *hospitalis* meaning 'hospitable', which in turn came from a word *hospes* meaning 'guest'. *Hospitalis* also gave us the word 'hospital' in the 14th century, when the word indeed meant a place of lodging for travellers. But centuries earlier, when the French had got hold of the Latin word *hospitalis*, they chewed on it as they tended to do and crunched it down by swallowing the middle syllable. By the time the English borrowed it from the French about 1250, it had become 'hostel'.

So 'hostel' was the standard word for a place of lodging for travellers from about 1300 to about 1550, but then died out. From 1400 on, people stayed in 'inns' (a word derived from the adverb 'in', being a place you stayed in), and 'inn' survived while 'hostel' disappeared from use. It wouldn't even exist in the language today had it not been revived by Sir Walter Scott in the 19th century.

But meanwhile, English was still not happy with having derived only two words from the Latin word *hospitalis*; it wanted another one. In the 1700s it became very trendy for young Englishmen to go on a tour of the continent, and by this time the French had taken their old word *hostel* and dropped the *s*, so that it had become *hôtel* in French. When the English trendies came back from the continent it would be terribly uncool to say, 'I stayed at an inn' when they instead could say, 'I stayed at an hotel in France' in a pretentious sort of way. The *h* wasn't pronounced in English for a couple of centuries, probably not until the beginning of the 20th century. This explains why you still sometimes see people write 'an hotel' in English, although there is absolutely no reason to do so. So there you go: we've got 'hotel' and 'hostel' and 'hospital', all from the same root. Then in the 19th century we made one last acquisition from this same root when we borrowed 'hospice' from the French.

Today, there is still one situation in which we, particularly in Canada, can see a living connection between hospitals and hotels. There are hospitals, in places like Kingston, Montreal, St Catharines, and Windsor, called the 'Hôtel-Dieu'. The 'hotel of God', what a bizarre name for a hospital, you think. But when you know the history, it isn't so bizarre.

HALLELUJAH!

❧

Easter is the time of year when you're sure to find a choir some-where singing many anthems and great baroque oratorios. You might hear one of Bach's *Passions* or Handel's *Messiah*, which was first performed at Easter, though now we tend to associate it with Christmas. It's an opportune time to look at some of these musical words.

EASTER

Eostre was an Anglo-Saxon goddess of the dawn, whose feast was celebrated at the vernal equinox. The early Christians had a habit of blending Christian with non-Christian practices; for instance, the date of Christmas coincides roughly with the Roman feast of Saturnalia (seven days of merrymaking, starting December 17) and the festival of the birth of the sun god Mithra (December 25). In this case, the Christian missionaries to Britain co-opted an Anglo-Saxon religious festival and even its name. In Romance languages, in contrast, the word for Easter is derived from the Hebrew word for Passover, *Pesach*; French, for instance, has *Pâques*.

ANTHEM

'Anthem', in the sense of a choral setting of a biblical text, has come a very long way, its ultimate origins being the Greek ele-ments *anti*, meaning 'against', and *phone,* meaning 'sound'. This became the church Latin word *antiphona,* meaning a composition sung with one choir responding to another, which has given us the word 'antiphon'.

But *antiphona* was fated to undergo another evolution. When the Anglo-Saxons were confronted with this church Latin word, they decided to drop a few syllables and thus turned *antiphona* into *antefne*. Even for the Anglo-Saxons, though, *antefne* was a hard mouthful of consonants, so gradually the *f* became an *m* and the final *ne* dropped off altogether, leaving us with 'antem' in the 15th century. Possibly because people thought the word was related to 'hymn', the *h* then crept in, establishing itself by about 1500. Throughout this time, 'anthem' maintained the original meaning of an antiphonal composition, but starting with Chaucer it also meant a piece of scripture set to music. Any singer who has recently made it through Holy Week can sympathize with the speaker in *Henry IV, Part 2*, who said, 'For my voice, I have lost it with hallowing, and singing of Anthems.'

Shakespeare also used the word more figuratively to mean any song of praise, and this led ultimately to its being used to describe the royalist song that gained popularity in the mid-1700s. But even in late Victorian times, pedants were complaining that 'anthem' was not the 'right' word for 'God Save the Queen', and that it should be called a 'national hymn' instead (as indeed national anthems are in French). This just shows that pedants never win in matters lexical. Just think how they would react to the latest evolution of the word, as in 'Technohead's irresistibly zany pro-marijuana anthem'. Definitely not suitable for Holy Week!

ORATORIO

Oratorios are so named in honour of the congregation of the Oratorians founded by St Philip Neri in the 16th century. It was St Philip who first had the idea of setting scenes from scripture to music in an attempt to interest young people in religion by making things a bit more dramatic—a 16th-century church youth group, if you like! Oratorios caught on in part because the opera houses had to be closed during Lent, and an oratorio provided both a kind of opera-substitute for the opera-mad Italians and employment for the opera singers and musicians during those eight weeks. The Oratorians themselves are so called because, in its early years, the congregation did its work from an oratory or chapel in a church in Rome rather than a church itself. The word 'oratory' is derived from the Latin words *oratorium templum*, meaning 'place for prayer'.

BAROQUE

The Portuguese word *barroco* designated irregularly shaped pearls, which were highly prized by Renaissance jewellers for their uniqueness. The word was borrowed into French in the 1500s as *baroque* and soon was extended beyond the realm of jewellery to describe anything odd or whimsical. It then came to apply to the new style of art and architecture, revelling in abnormality, distortion, and ornamentation, which replaced the sober correctness of Renaissance classicism. The word 'baroque' was always somewhat derogatory and confined to art history until the late 19th century, at which time it started to be applied to 17th- and 18th-century music as well as art and architecture.

PASSACAGLIA

A very famous piece of baroque music is Bach's *Passacaglia and Fugue in C Minor* for organ. Little did Bach know, probably, that the word 'passacaglia' came (through Italian) from two Spanish words, *pasar* meaning 'to walk' and *calle* meaning 'street'. The Spanish *passacalle* was a 17th-century dance of somewhat ill repute, performed in the streets.

TWEEDLEDUM AND TWEEDLEDEE

Baroque music is also, surprisingly, the source of the expression 'Tweedledum and Tweedledee', which we tend to associate with *Through the Looking-Glass*. But calling two indistinguishable people or things 'tweedledum and tweedledee' is actually older than

Lewis Carroll. In 1725 the English writer John Byrom coined the expression to satirize the music of Handel and another composer, Bononcini, who sounds like a small kind of mozzarella cheese but was in fact a highly prolific composer in the early 1700s who rivalled Handel in popularity. And when you think about how baroque music sounds, 'tweedledum and tweedledee' describes it very well! Of course, if you are listening to a Bach or Handel oratorio, I hope the only word that comes to mind to describe it is 'sublime'.

EASTER BONNETS

ॐ

Easter has traditionally been a time to acquire a new hat, so in this section we look at the word 'bonnet' and other names for headgear.

BONNET
'Bonnet' comes from an Old French word *bonet*, which seems to have been a kind of material, because we find references to *chapels de bonet* or 'hats made of "bonet"'. This might have been a Germanic word, related to 'bind' and 'bundle'. Alternatively, there was also a Late Latin word *abonnis*, designating a ribbon used in headgear. Originally a bonnet was a type of headgear for men, as in a Scottish bonnet, because in the early Middle Ages women tended to wear veils rather than hats. But it eventually came to apply only to women's hats and now only to babies' hats.

HAT, HOOD, CAP
Hat and hood are ultimately related Germanic words, because for a long time the most common type of head covering was a hood

rather than a hat. Likewise, 'cap' comes from a Latin word for a hooded cloak, *cappa*, which has also given us 'cape'. As a piece of headgear detached from a cloak, a cap was female headgear before it was used for men, but by 1571 we find a very interesting statute passed by Elizabeth I to the effect that 'Every person shall wear upon the Sabbath and holy day upon their head a Cap of Wooll knit thicked and dressed in England.' This was obviously the result of intense lobbying by the English cap makers!

BERET

Hooded capes are also involved in the history of the word 'beret'. A Latin word for such a cape was *birrus*, which also gave us *biretta*, the four-cornered hat formerly worn by Catholic priests. *Béret* came into French from the dialect of Béarn, a province in the southwest of France, in the 19th century. It is a Béarnais word because the type of cap was originally worn by Basque peasants. Berets must have burst upon the fashionable scene after the defeat of Napoleon, because the word first shows up in French in 1819 and was being used in English only eight years later to designate a fashionable ladies' hat made of black velvet and trimmed with gold lace. The Basque peasants would have been surprised!

FEDORA, TAM

These are both named after literary characters. Fedora was a character in a play of the same name by Victorien Sardou, a wildly successful 19th-century French playwright who also wrote the play on which the opera *Tosca* is based. Now, Fedora was a female (she was played by Sarah Bernhardt) and I haven't been able to find out whether she wore the hat, which is now more typically a man's hat.

'Tam' comes from 'Tam O'Shanter', a poem by Robbie Burns, the hero of which would have been called 'Tom of Shanter' in English. A tam is, of course, originally a Scottish hat, apparently

worn particularly by ploughmen (Tam in the poem is a farmer)—
the 1790s equivalent of the John Deere hat, I guess!

BOWLER

The bowler hat is so called not because it looks like a bowl but
because it was designed in 1850 by an English hatter called
William Bowler.

MILLINERY

'Milliner' was originally the name for a native of Milan, or as it was
pronounced in English in the Middle Ages, MILLEN. Milan was
renowned, then as now, as a fashion centre, and particularly for
producing fancy textiles and trim. Milan lace was a big item, as
were other accessories. By the 1500s, 'milliner' was being used to
mean a person who sold these fancy wares. Hats are a major acces-
sory, so eventually 'milliner' got narrowed down to someone who
sells or makes hats.

BIRDS OF A FEATHER

∞

The American naturalist and renowned bird painter John James
Audubon was born on 26 April, 1785, and to honour him and the
return of birds in the spring, let us look at the names of some
birds, as well as a phrase that has its origins in the name of a bird.

WHISKY JACK

The Canada jay is also known as the 'grey jay', or, more pic-
turesquely, the 'camp robber', because of its notorious boldness in
stealing food from camps. But it is also known as a 'whisky jack',

a name that has nothing to do with alcohol consumption, but rather has its origins in Cree or Montagnais, both Algonquian languages. In those languages, the name of this bird is *wiskatjan*. *Wiskatjan* also meant 'blacksmith', and apparently the bird was called this because of its sooty grey colour. The English newcomers (most likely the employees of the Hudson's Bay Company) in the 18th century assimilated this word into English, heard *wiskatjan,* and called it 'whisky John'. As you might expect, it was a short step to make it more familiar, by using the nickname 'Jack' for 'John', so 'whisky john' ended up as 'whisky jack'.

PTARMIGAN

You would think that this word would also be derived from some northern Aboriginal language in Canada. In fact, it comes from a Gaelic word, *tàrmachan*, which meant 'grumbler' or 'croaker', presumably in reference to the sound the bird makes. In Gaelic, as you see, there was no 'p' at the beginning of the word, so if we'd just stuck with the Scottish name, life (or at least spelling) would be so much easier. But in the late 17th century, some meddlesome person, thinking the word was derived from Greek (as was their wont back then), stuck a 'p' at the beginning, as if it were related to 'pterodactyl' or some of those Greek words. We ended up stuck with it, though there is absolutely no good reason for having a 'p' at the beginning of this word, making it so difficult to spell and confusing to pronounce. Thank goodness they didn't get hold of the Canada…pgoose!

LOON

'Loon', the bird, is a corruption of *loom*, a Scottish word that came from Old Norse for this particular bird. The Scottish origin is not surprising because, in the British Isles, this bird is found only in Scotland. But you're going to want to know, is this related to the loom that we weave on?

Actually that's a different word altogether. In Anglo-Saxon, *loom* meant any tool or device. Amusingly, it went through a phase from about 1400 to 1600 when it was used to mean 'penis' (it did after all mean 'tool'!). It came to mean the device for weaving about 1500.

ALBATROSS

'Albatross' seems to be a corruption of the Spanish word *alcatraz*, which was applied to various seabirds, such as the gannet or the pelican. The name of the famous penitentiary comes from the island on which it sits, called by the Spanish 'the island of the pelicans'. The Spanish in turn adopted the word from Arabic, where *al* means 'the' and *qadus* designated the white-tailed sea eagle. So this word has kicked around several languages and been applied to several large white seabirds. Finally in English it settled down as the very large sea bird immortalized as an ill omen in Coleridge's 'The Rime of the Ancient Mariner'. *Alcatraz* changed to 'albatross' under the influence of the Latin *albus*, meaning 'white'.

PELICAN

This comes from the Greek word *pelekus*, meaning an axe, and its derivative *pelekan*, meaning 'hew with an axe', probably referring to the shape of its bill.

PARTRIDGE

When partridges are scared, they take flight with a loud cackle and whirring sound made by their wings. For this reason, the ancient Greeks called the bird a *perdix*, which was related to their verb *perdesthai*, meaning 'to break wind'. And if you go even further back than Greek, into Indo-European, you find the root *perd*, meaning 'to break wind', which migrated down through Greek and Latin and French and English as 'partridge', but also migrated through Germanic into English, undergoing a few consonant and vowel changes along the way, to give us the word 'fart'!

WAXWING
The waxwing has small red tips on the end of the secondary feathers of its wings, which look like blobs of sealing wax.

HALCYON DAYS
The ancient Greeks' name for the kingfisher was *alcyon*. This derived from a mythological character called Alcyone, a daughter of Aeolus the wind god. She and her husband, Ceyx, were noted for their love and devotion, and the story goes that when Ceyx was drowned at sea, the gods took pity on her and reunited them as birds, she as a kingfisher and he as a tern. There was a charming belief that the kingfisher bred at the winter solstice and brooded on a nest floating on the water. Aeolus, out of love for his transformed daughter, magically charmed the wind and the waves so that they were particularly calm at this time of year. So a period of calm weather around the winter solstice was known as the 'halcyon days'. Of course, now it means any calm or peaceful time, especially with connotations of happiness and prosperity.

THE TAX MAN COMETH

&

In April you may well be contemplating your income tax return, which may in turn have you thinking about various words to designate your hard-earned cash, or, as Mr Micawber in *David Copperfield* would have said, your 'pecuniary emoluments'. Let us hope that, when all is said and done, and the various governments have been appeased, you do not find yourself bankrupt!

SALARY

Most of us would just call our 'pecuniary emoluments' our salary, a word that is, surprisingly, related to salt. In the ancient world, salt was a very important commodity as a preservative for meat and fish, and Roman soldiers were given a special allowance to buy it. The Latin name for this allowance was *salarium*, meaning 'pertaining to salt', *sal* being the Latin word for salt. Eventually *salarium* came to apply to the soldiers' regular pay. The word came into English via the Normans in the 14th century.

PAY

And speaking of 'pay', when you get your cheque (or more likely your electronic bank deposit) on payday, you are literally being 'appeased' by your employer: the word 'pay' derives ultimately (and surprisingly) from the Latin word *pax*, meaning peace. This is how it happened. There was a verb in Latin *pacare*, derived from pax, which meant 'pacify'. Specifically it was applied not to pacifying babies or warlike tribes, but to pacifying people you owed money to, the only way to do that being to give them the money! So *pacare* came to mean 'give money to'—'pay', in fact. It came into English via French after the Norman invasion.

PITTANCE

You may be thinking that what is left from your pay after you've 'pacified' the various governments with all your taxes is a mere pittance. This comes from the Latin word *pietas*, the same word that has given us 'pity' and 'piety'. A pittance was originally, in the Middle Ages, a pious bequest or donation to a religious order. This bequest had a particular purpose: it paid for a little extra wine or food for the monks or nuns on the anniversary of the donor's death. It wasn't a huge amount, maybe just one glass of wine, or a small treat, so that by the late Middle Ages 'pittance' meant also any small portion of food or drink. By the early 1700s it came to mean a small allowance or means of livelihood, with the emphasis on the scantiness of the remuneration.

WAGE

'Wage' is another word we owe to the Normans. It meant a pledge, a token of loyalty, or something given as security. So the word 'wage' underlines the contractual relationship of loyalty between employer and employee. The same Germanic word that gave us 'wage' also gave us 'gage' as in 'a gage of my affection'. This is another case where the Anglo-Normans could pronounce an initial *w* sound in words coming from Germanic, but the central French had to stick a *g* before it.

All of these words for money given in exchange for work—wage, salary, pay—come from the Norman French conquerors of England. This is not surprising, because French was the language of the administration after the Conquest, and it would have been the French speakers who had the money to employ people. The Anglo-Saxon word that all these words supplanted was *meed*.

INCOME TAX

As you sharpen your pencil, it is probably no consolation for you to learn that the term 'income tax' has been with us since 1799, when income tax was first introduced as a fund-raising measure during the Napoleonic Wars.

DOLLAR

To find the origins of the word 'dollar', we have to go back to Bohemia in the 1500s. In 1516, a silver mine opened in a place called Joachimsthal, which means 'St Joachim's Valley' in German. By 1519, they were minting large silver coins there, which were called *Joachimsthalergulden,* or 'guilders from Joachimsthal'. These coins, or coins like them, were used throughout Germany, and since *Joachimsthalergulden* was a bit of a mouthful, it got shortened to *thaler* (pronounced like TALLER). By the 1550s, this word had been borrowed into English as 'dollar', and was used to designate not only German and Scandinavian coins, but also the Spanish peso or 'piece of eight' (eight *reales*), which was formerly used throughout the Spanish colonies in the New World and largely in British North America just before the American Revolution. The use of 'two bits' to mean twenty-five cents is a holdover from this time when the basic monetary unit was divided into eight parts or bits: two bits was equal to a quarter-dollar. When the Continental Congress had to decide what to call the new American monetary unit in 1785, they called it a dollar, because the term was already so well known. Canada adopted the decimal monetary system and the name 'dollar' in 1858.

CASH

The word 'cash' came into English from French *casse* (now *caisse*) or Italian *cassa* in the 1500s, and, like those words, meant a box for money. Almost immediately it also came to mean the money itself; there is a reference to cash in this sense in Shakespeare's *Henry V.* It is unclear why the word ends in a *sh* sound in English (it always has), since it ends in *ss* in the languages from which it is borrowed. An interesting development of this word in Canada is that it is used to mean a cash register or cash desk, as in 'Please pay at the front cash'. Indeed, Canadians travelling abroad are well-advised to be aware of this, lest an innocent query such as 'Where's the cash?' may lead one's interlocutor to think they are being held up!

DIME

'Dime' comes to us ultimately from the Latin *decima* meaning 'one-tenth', which got scrunched down in Old French to *disme*, and subsequently to *dime*. This word was used in Old French (and still is today in Modern French) as well as medieval English to mean the tithe, or one-tenth of one's goods paid to the church or a ruler as a tax. The word had died out but was revived by the Americans when they named their dollar in 1785.

NICKEL

Nickel was discovered by a Swedish mineralogist, Axel von Cronstedt, who isolated the substance from an ore in 1751. This ore had been previously known to German miners, who called it *Kupfernickel,* from the German words *Kupfer* meaning 'copper' and *Nickel* meaning a rascal or mischievous demon. They called it this because it looked like copper ore but actually yielded no copper. So when von Cronstedt had to come up with a name for his new discovery, he called it 'nickel'. The word came to be applied to a coin in 1857. At that time, a nickel was an American one-cent coin containing twelve percent nickel. From 1864, pennies were instead made of bronze. In 1866, nickel made its way back into coinage, this time in a five-cent coin that was twenty-five percent nickel.

BUCK

We do not know why 'buck' is a slang term for 'dollar'. It may have derived from the 18th-century practice of using buckskins as a unit of exchange. This explanation is not all that far-fetched: an analogous example was the 'beaver', the standard unit of exchange in Canada of the fur trade era, equivalent in value to the cost of one beaver pelt. Our first written evidence of 'buck', however, doesn't appear till 1856, quite some time after the use of buckskins as currency had fallen out of favour (just think how difficult it would be to fit one in your wallet).

The expression 'pass the buck' derives from a different word 'buck', the origin of which is also obscure. A 'buck' was an inanimate object placed before the person whose turn it was to deal at poker. So passing the buck was passing on responsibility. The earliest evidence we have for 'pass the buck' is from Jack London in 1908.

BREAD
In the slang sense, 'bread' meaning 'money' is very recent, dating from the mid-20th century. But the word has been around for a very long time. In Old English, the word 'bread' meant 'a piece, a morsel'. The word the Anglo-Saxons used for the food made of leavened flour that we call bread was 'loaf', and early translations of the Gospels have Jesus saying, 'I am the loaf of life.' So you would ask for a 'bread of loaf' rather than a 'piece of bread'. But between 800 and about 1200, the word 'bread' passed through a series of sense shifts from 'piece', to 'piece of bread', to 'broken bread', to designate what we know now as bread. Meanwhile, 'loaf' became restricted to a single item of bread.

BANK, BANKRUPT
'Bank' comes from Italian *banca* or *banco*, the bench or table on which moneylenders conducted business (the Italians, especially the Lombards, invented modern banking during the Renaissance). If one of those Italians was unable to pay his creditors, it was said that his bench was broken or wrecked, *banca rotta*. The French adopted this as *banqueroute*, and when the English borrowed it in the 1500s, they gave it a false Latin ending based on *ruptus,* meaning broken. 'Bankrupt' originally meant the state of being insolvent (one would talk about being 'cast into bankrupt'), but when 'bankrupt' came to apply to the insolvent person himself, the language had to come up with another word for the insolvent state. Over two centuries English experimented with 'bankrupting', 'bankruption', 'bankrupture', and 'bankruptship' before settling on 'bankruptcy' in about 1700.

Bringing Down the Budget

&

Once your friendly provincial and federal governments have relieved you of your money, they announce how they are going to spend it by bringing down their annual budget, an event that usually happens, in Ontario at least, in late April or early May.

BUDGET

There are two distinctively Canadian words we use when talking about a government budget. One is the verb 'bring down': we talk about the government bringing down the budget. This usage is now found only in Canada, Australia, and New Zealand. It was used in England also in the 19th century but seems to have died out there. The second is the word 'lockup' for the situation of journalists who are locked away with the budget documents just before the budget is brought down in the house. As far as we know, this usage is uniquely Canadian. Visitors to Canada at budget time must think we are terribly undemocratic when they hear that we have thrown our journalists in the lockup!

The word 'budget' itself is related to both 'bulge' and 'bilge'. It all started with a Gaulish word for a leather pouch that the Romans borrowed as *bulga*. In Old French this got turned into *bouge*, and a small bag was therefore a *bougette*. This could be a money bag, or a pouch for a peddler's wares. This word came into English in the 1400s, in various spellings, among them 'budget'. A phrase arose in the 1500s, 'to open one's budget' meaning to say what was on one's mind. By the 1700s, this phrase was being used of the Chancellor of the Exchequer making his annual statement, as if he were opening up his money bag for all to see. By the end of the 1700s, 'budget' was being used independently of the phrase 'open one's budget', and by the mid-1800s 'budget' was being used of household financial plans as well as government ones.

But how is 'budget' connected with 'bulge' and 'bilge'? Well, this same French word *bouge* had a variant *boulge*, and since the meaning of *boulge* was a round bag, there arose a verb *boulger* meaning to swell up, to take on the form of a pouch. One of the rounded protuberant things that the noun 'bulge' (as the English spelled *boulge*) applied to was the bottom of a ship's hull. But soon in this sense 'bulge' got corrupted to 'bilge'. And we use 'bilge' to mean rubbish because the interior of a ship's hull accumulates a lot of garbage. So if you feel that some government's latest budget is bilge, you're just being etymologically consistent!

FISCAL

The adjective meaning 'related to public revenue' is 'fiscal'. It comes from a now rare noun, 'fisc', which meant the royal or state treasury. This came from the Latin word for the public treasury of Rome, *fiscus*, which was derived from a word meaning a woven basket.

FINANCE

'Finance' comes ultimately from the Latin *finis* meaning 'end', and from the Old French verb derived from that, *finer*, which meant 'to end', and in particular to settle a debt so that it is ended. Nowadays, when you finance your house or your car, it doesn't feel as though you're putting an end to your debt at all. It feels like you're extending your debt forever and ever! But that's what it meant in the Middle Ages: the finance was the final payment on a loan. It could also be used as a ransom for a feudal lord. This was something, apparently, that had to be financed fairly frequently. You have to wonder whether if, back then, instead of having the mortgage rates posted in the banks, they had the 'feudal lord's ransom rates' posted. Not surprisingly, the word was also used to mean the payment of one's taxes, which is another kind of debt in a way. This is why we talk about the Department of Finance and the finance minister.

EXCHEQUER

In England the minister of finance is known as the Chancellor of the Exchequer. 'Exchequer' comes to us from checkers! Under the Norman kings of England, the accounts of the royal revenue were kept by a system where counters were placed on a checkered cloth, similar to a chess board. I doubt that Revenue Canada uses this system. The Old French word for chess was *eschecs*, which was derived ultimately from a Persian word *shah mat* which meant 'the king is dead' (*shah* meaning 'king' in Persian). *Shah mat* is the ultimate origin of our word 'checkmate'. And *eschequier* was the name for a chessboard. Because this accounting table looked like a chessboard, it too became known as an 'escheker'.

ECONOMY

The economy is, of course, a constant preoccupation for the minister of finance. 'Economy' comes from two Greek words, *oikos* meaning 'house' and *nomos* meaning 'management', and originally meant 'household management'. This literal sense survives only in 'home economics', which really is the study of household management, but I'm not even sure it survives there, since 'home ec' has now been replaced by 'human ecology' and 'family studies'.

But 'household management' is what 'economy' meant when it came into English in the 1500s, and we even have a quotation from the poet Andrew Marvell saying 'You have, contrary to… good economy made a snow-house in your upper room'—which you can see would not be good household management!

Because a major part of household management is managing the money, in another hundred years 'economy' came to mean managing the resources of organizations larger than households, even of countries, and finally came to apply to the wealth and resources themselves.

DEBT

'Debt' has a fairly straightforward etymology, but it is the spelling which is interesting. Why does it have a silent *b*? It comes from the Latin *debitum*, which meant 'something owing'. The French scrunched this down so that by the 1100s the *b* was lost and they were left with *dette*. This is what the English borrowed in about 1300. For about 200 years we quite happily spelled it 'dett' or 'dette'. But then, in the Renaissance, people started looking at Latin again and said, 'Aha! This comes from the Latin word *debitum,* so it should have a *b* in it too.' So since about Tudor times we've been stuck with this totally unnecessary *b*. The French went through a phase like this too, trying to spell it *debte,* but they were smarter and reverted to *dette*. And we're left with another silly English spelling.

OPENING UP THE COTTAGE

☯

Victoria Day weekend (or 'May Two-Four' weekend as it's known in Ontario) is the traditional time for Canadians to open up their cottages. Even though cottaging is a classic Canadian activity from coast to coast, it's quite surprising how many different names there are for the summer residence.

COTTAGE

'Cottage' comes from an Old English word *cot* or *cote* meaning a humble dwelling. *Cote* has survived in 'dovecote'. 'Cottage' was an Anglo-Norman derivative of this; just as we have 'bag' and 'baggage', a cottage was a *cot* along with its various appurtenances, like a yard for the chickens. For a very long time the word 'cottage' was restricted to humble labourers' dwellings. It was almost a legal term for such a house. So a cottage was definitely not something that the middle class or the wealthy would aspire to. Then, in the mid-1700s, along came Jean-Jacques Rousseau to change all that. Now, I'm sure most people barrelling down (or crawling along) the highway to their luxurious Muskoka retreat don't think they owe anything to an 18th-century philosopher, but they do. Rousseau spearheaded the Pre-Romantic movement, which rejected the grandiose, sophisticated, refined, and often artificial ideals of the classical age and promoted a simpler lifestyle with an appreciation of nature. So there was a kind of back-to-nature movement in the mid-to-late-1700s, exemplified by Marie-Antoinette playing at being a shepherdess at the bucolic retreat she had built in the grounds of Versailles. It became trendy at that time for the English gentry and wealthy middle class to have a smaller and simpler country house to which they could retreat from their mansions in town, and with a kind of inverse snobbery they called these 'cottages'. It was in North America in the 1880s that the name came to be applied specifically to summer residences by a lake. 'Cottage Country' is a Canadianism.

CAMP

In Northern Ontario and parts of the Maritimes, people call their summer home a 'camp'. 'Camp' comes to us from the Latin word *campus,* meaning a field, and more specifically (academics take note!) a field of battle with all the troops lodged in tents or other temporary accommodation. From the military sense the word also came to be applied to other temporary or makeshift lodgings, as in a lumber camp. It is probably because of the prevalence of lumber camps and fishing camps in Northern Ontario and New Brunswick that the word came to be applied to one's 'temporary' summer lodging as well.

CABIN

This is what many Westerners call their cottage. It comes from a popular Latin word for 'hut', *capanna*. When it came into English from French in the 1400s it really did designate something rudimentary and makeshift. In the Middle Ages, a cabin was even lower down on the social scale than a cottage. It was usually a hovel built of sod.

CHALET

In Quebec, cottages are often called 'chalets', which evokes visions of Heidi in the Alps. Not surprisingly, the word comes from Swiss French. It may be a diminutive of the Old French word for a farmstead, *chasel*, which in turn came from the Latin word for 'house', *casa*. Alternatively, it could come from a pre-Roman word *cala,* meaning 'shelter'. Now, by an amazing coincidence, Jean-Jacques Rousseau is involved in this one too. It was he who popularized this Swiss word (being Swiss himself) in standard French, by using it in his novel *La Nouvelle Héloïse*, which was incredibly popular in the 18th century, a huge bestseller (for reasons which I have to say escape me, having had to plough my way through it as an undergraduate). It depicted an idealized happy prosperous countryside. By the mid-1800s the French too had adopted the idea of having a country house by the sea (facilitated in large part by the advent of the railway, which made it easy for Parisians to get to the beaches of Normandy), and I guess it was in the hope that their country resort would have the same idyllic rustic charm as that depicted in *La Nouvelle Héloïse* that they called it a *chalet*.

BUNGALOW

In Cape Breton, a summer cottage is called a 'bungalow', which is a word of South Asian origin (see DIWALI, page 128).

SHACK

In Newfoundland and parts of the Maritimes, summer residences—even luxurious ones—can be called 'shacks'. This seems to be a North American back-formation from *shackle,* meaning 'ramshackle', which in turn was an adjective derived from an Old English verb 'shack', meaning 'to shake'.

THE RAKE'S PROGRESS

☙

Victoria Day weekend is also the traditional time to plant one's garden. It is striking how many words related to the actions and tools associated with gardening, including the word 'garden' itself, go all the way back to Old English without any change of meaning.

Some examples are 'spade', 'rake', 'hoe', 'barrow' (as in 'wheelbar-row'), 'grass', 'clover', 'hedge', 'tree', 'plant', 'shrub', 'mow', 'dig', and 'weed' (yes, they really have been around forever!). The word 'fork' was used for centuries to designate the garden tool before it became the eating implement. But some gardening terms are newer and have indeed gone through changes in meaning.

LAWN

'Lawn' entered the language in the 1500s meaning a clearing in the woods, as a variant of *laund* meaning 'glade'. *Laund* came into English in the 1300s from an Old French word *launde* (Modern French *lande*) meaning a moor or heath, which in turn came from an Old Celtic word which is related to the Germanic word that gave us 'land'. Medieval gardens in England do seem to have included lawns, but they were probably called 'flowery meads'. I think we should revive this, because it would be so great to buy a 'flowery mead mower'! By the late 1600s 'lawn' had come to mean a stretch of land left untilled and therefore likely to be covered with grass. In the early 1700s, garden design for the stately mansions in England changed to a more natural, less formal style, which incorporated large expanses of grass kept short (usually by sheep!). The word 'lawn' was just waiting for a job opportunity and there it was, thanks to the 18th-century garden designers who developed the classic English garden.

MANURE

'Manure' is older as a verb than as a noun and had nothing to do with dung to start with! It comes from Old French *manouvrer*, the same word that gave us 'manoeuvre', which came from the Latin *manu operari* meaning 'to work with the hand'. In Old French, *manouvrer* meant to hold or occupy land or property and subsequently to administer or manage. When the English borrowed the word in the 1400s, it meant to cultivate land, but it could also be used figuratively to mean to cultivate or train the body, mind, or spirit. For instance, around 1550 we find a quotation as follows: 'Those Scotts which inhabit the Southe, being farre the best parte, are well manured', and in 1607 a prayer imploring God to 'manure our work without, and prepare our minds within'. I haven't heard anyone asking to be covered with manure lately! Since cultivating plants required the application of dung (the word that had been used since Old English times to mean a mixture of excrement and decaying vegetation used as fertilizer), 'manure' soon came to mean fertilizing the land in this way and the substance used as a fertilizer.

COMPOST
This comes from the same Latin root as 'compose', 'composite', and 'composure': *componere*, meaning 'put together'. *Compostum* was the past participle: 'something that has been put together'. *Compostum* did have the meaning of green fertilizer in medieval Latin, but when the word was borrowed into English in the 1400s, it didn't yet have only this specific sense. Rather, composts could be mixtures of various sorts, for example a stew, or a preserve of fruit and spice in wine. A recipe from the 1450s talks about 'pears in compost', which sounds distinctly unappetizing. The fertilizer sense dates from around the same time but is the only sense to survive.

POLLEN
The Latin word *pollen* meant 'fine dust' or 'finely-ground flour'. It was the botanist Linnaeus who, in 1751, applied it to the powdery fertilizing substance in flowers.

ALLERGY, HAY FEVER
'Allergy' is not a gardening word, but it's hard to mention the word 'pollen' without thinking about it. The word was coined in German

in 1906 by an Austrian pediatrician, who was the first to use it in English, in 1911. He coined it from two Greek words, *allos,* meaning 'different', and the end of the word 'energy', to mean 'reactivity'.

Now, one has to ask, surely people had allergies before 1906? And indeed they did: medical history has reports of cat and egg allergies and asthma attacks as far back as the 1600s. An Italian doctor of the mid-1500s first made the connection with plants by observing the sneezing and itching suffered by a patient whenever he was exposed to roses. The affliction went by the name of 'rose-cold', 'rose-fever', or 'rose-catarrh' for some time. In the 19th century it was also known as 'summer catarrh', but in the 1820s we begin to see references to 'hay asthma' or 'hay fever'. Medical discoveries in the mid-1800s confirmed that grass and other pollens were responsible. Indeed, the physician who fingered pollen as the culprit advised his patients to avoid it by spending the summer on a peninsula or… a yacht. I wonder whether medicare would cover that! But this probably helped to establish 'hay fever' as the standard term.

GOOD STUFF CHEAP

&

As summer looms on the horizon, it's time to do some spring cleaning and clear out some clutter through a garage sale or rummage sale.

GARAGE (SALE)
Our first quotation for 'garage sale' is fairly recent, from 1966, but 'garage' (for which we have seven different pronunciations in the *Canadian Oxford Dictionary*) came to us from French at the begin-

ning of the 20th century. In French it is derived from *garer*, meaning to park a car. It had not always meant that, however. It had survived for many centuries on the margins of the French language as a verb for mooring a boat in a sheltered spot. It was adapted to use in reference to bicycles in 1868 and subsequently to cars. Ultimately, it comes from a Germanic word *waron*, meaning 'protect' or 'be careful with'. As I have mentioned before, Old French always changed an initial *w* to *g*, and this is why *waron* became *garer* in French. But in English we also have an offspring of this Germanic word: it's our word 'ware', as in 'beware' and 'wary'. And the other 'ware', as an item for sale, also started out life meaning 'an object one took care of'. So if you're wary about the wares at a garage sale, you're just being etymologically consistent!

RUMMAGE

The word 'rummage', which we borrowed from the French in the early 1500s, originally meant the arranging of barrels and so on in the hold of ship. By the 1600s, it had become a verb meaning to search thoroughly through the hold of a ship, to ransack the contents of the hold, especially if you were a customs officer looking for smuggled goods. Not rum, necessarily. Rum has nothing to do with rummage, lest you are on your way to creating a folk etymology. In another hundred years, it came to mean 'search out' or 'dig out' in any context, what you do when you are cleaning out your house. In the 19th century, a rummage sale was first of all a type of clearance sale of goods left at docks or in warehouses. It then became the charity sale of second-hand goods that we know today.

FLEA MARKET

Since about 1890 there has been an outdoor market in Paris called the *Marché aux Puces*—which means literally 'flea market'—selling second-hand goods, especially clothes. It is presumed that, especially when the market first appeared and people's hygiene was less than exemplary, many of these items were infested with fleas, and this is where the name came from.

CHEAP

'Cheap' surprisingly started out in life as a noun rather than an adjective. Way back in Anglo-Saxon times, 'cheap', or 'chap', as it was then pronounced, meant 'buying and selling'—trade, in effect. It is ultimately derived from a Latin word *caupo,* meaning a trades-man or tavern keeper. The pronunciation CHAP has survived in the name Chapman, which was a medieval word meaning 'pedlar', and in 'chapbook', which was a small book sold by chapmen.

After a few hundred years of meaning 'trade', the emphasis of the word 'cheap' shifted more to the transaction from the pur-chaser's point of view, and by the 1300s 'cheap' began to mean a purchase, especially a bargain. The phrases 'good cheap' and 'great cheap' arose to mean, essentially, a great bargain—a bargoon, to use a Canadianism. So there were sentences like 'Food is good cheap in London', meaning it was inexpensive (something no one is likely to say in this day and age!). Gradually people ceased to recognize it as a noun and came to think it was an adjective. As a result, the adjective took over and the noun died out altogether by the 18th century, until the phrase 'on the cheap' arose in the mid-1800s.

KNICK-KNACK

'Knick-knack' is what we call a reduplication. Reduplication also happens in words like 'mishmash', 'shilly-shally', and so on. In the case of 'knick-knack', the word being reduplicated was 'knack', which we use now to mean a particular skill at doing something. But 'knack' did not always mean this. At its origins in Chaucer's time, it meant a kind of trick, especially a deceitful or underhand-ed way of getting something. The idea of ingeniousness was very important, and by Shakespeare's time 'knack' could also mean a kind of clever gadget or a toy, especially a small or trivial one. A century later, by the 1680s, 'knack' had been reduplicated into 'knick-knack' with the current sense of a trinket or ornament. There must have been a great vogue for knick-knacks after that, because for about a century, from 1700 on, we actually had a word 'knick-knackatory', meaning a place full of knick-knacks, and 'knick-knackatorian', meaning a person who sold them.

WHITE ELEPHANT

The story goes that in Thailand white elephants were considered sacred, and the kings of Thailand, if they wanted to ruin a courtier, would make him a gift of a white elephant, knowing that the upkeep would be ruinous but that the courtier could not refuse such a generous gift. From this came the notion of something expensive but useless that one is anxious to get rid of, an early 20th-century usage. Nowadays, white-elephant tables at rummage sales offer items that are cheap but useless.

A MATTER OF DEGREE

&

The beginning of summer coincides with university graduation.
Stairs, concrete, and (yes, again) cows are all part of the story.

GRADUATE, GRADUATION, DEGREE
'Graduation' comes from the Latin word for 'a step in a flight of
stairs', *gradus*. This has given English many words, among them
'gradual'. There is one surviving usage in English in which 'gradual'
has retained the literal sense of *gradus*. In some Christian liturgies,
there is something called a 'gradual psalm'. I used to think it was
called that because it can seem to go on forever, but actually it is
because originally this psalm was sung from the steps of the altar.
In medieval university Latin, *gradus* also meant a figurative step in
the process of acquiring an academic education, and *graduare*
meant to acknowledge the achievement of each of those stages. So
by the late 1400s there was an anglicized version of this, 'graduate',
which meant a person who had achieved the first stage of his edu-

cation. The verb 'graduate', meaning to confer a university degree on someone, came a century later.

'Degree' is simply a doublet of this Latin word: it came through French rather than directly from Latin. A *degradus* in Latin was a step down, and as usual the French dropped a few consonants until it ended up as 'degree'. For several hundred years after it came into English in the 1200s, 'degree' meant literally a step, but, just like *gradus*, the word acquired figurative meanings, so that by the 1300s it was also used to mean the stages of a university education.

GRADE

To graduate and get your degree, you have to have good grades, and 'grade' is yet another word derived from *gradus*. The French version of *gradus*—*grade*—lingered on the edges of the English language from about 1500 to about 1800, meaning one of the 360 degrees in a circle. Then, for some reason, in about 1800 it too started to be used to mean a step or stage in a process. Shortly after that it started being used, in the United States only, to mean a year of schooling. By the late 1800s it was being used for the marks indicating a student's level of achievement. One of the shibboleths that Canadians use to identify Americans is that they refer to grades in school with ordinals (fourth grade), whereas we prefer cardinal numbers (Grade Four).

MARK

The marks we get in school literally started out as marks of a pen. (The word 'mark' itself designating a sign of some kind goes back to Old English times.) The practice in the 18th or 19th century was to keep a register of students' names and, for every correct answer or something else meritorious, the teacher would make a mark next to the student's name. The total number of marks was totted up and determined each student's rank in the class.

DIPLOMA

'Diploma' ultimately comes from a Greek word meaning 'a doubling', which was used for a paper folded in half. It then came to mean an official document conferring a privilege, and this is the sense it had when it came into English in the mid-1600s, originally as a state charter. This is why diplomats are called 'diplomats', because originally they had one of these 'diplomas' conferring official status on them. But very soon after that it came to mean what we know it as now—a document conferring a degree.

PARCHMENT

'Parchment' came to us via French from the Latin word *pergamena*, which meant 'writing material from Pergamum'. Pergamum (which was in what is now Turkey) was the capital of an ancient kingdom and a splendid centre of Hellenistic culture in the 2nd and 3rd centuries BC. It had one of the greatest libraries in the ancient world, so it's not surprising that the Pergamites were very interested in writing materials. In the 2nd century BC they developed a new improved method of cleaning, stretching, and scraping the skins of animals—usually sheep, goats, and calves—so that they could be written on. This upgrade in the operating system, so to speak, was so much of an improvement that both sides could be written on, making possible the production of bound books instead of rolled scrolls. The Pergamites should have patented this invention, because parchment was *the* writing material in Europe until the invention of the printing press sixteen centuries later! What we call parchment today is not real animal-skin parchment but just a fine paper made from wood pulp and rags. And the parchment paper much beloved by cookie bakers for its non-stick properties is ordinary paper soaked in dilute sulphuric acid. The use of 'parchment' to mean a university diploma dates from the 1850s.

BACHELOR

'Bachelor' may ultimately be derived from the Latin word for 'cow'. This was *vacca,* which in late Latin was transformed into *bacca.* (This kind of transformation is quite understandable if you listen to Spanish, where the letter *b* is pronounced halfway between a *b* and a *v.*) It is thought that a *baccalarius* was a person employed on the Roman equivalent of a cattle ranch to look after the cows. From there the word took a leap, we're not quite sure how, to mean a young knight in the service of another, and also a junior member of a trade guild—basically the person at the bottom of the hierarchy. By the mid-1300s it was already being used to mean the person who has taken the lowest degree at a university. In every sense, the word described someone who was in a process of training: a knight who was training to be a better knight, an apprentice in a trade, or a young person training to be an academic. But at about the same time it started to be used of unmarried men, who I suppose could be considered to be in training to be married men. Our first quotation in that sense is from the *Canterbury Tales*: 'Bachelors have often pain and woe.' That was what Chaucer thought about bachelordom, I guess!

There is a distinctly Canadian use of 'bachelor', to designate a studio apartment with combined living/dining/bedroom. I always think tourists must find it entertaining, as they walk down Canadian streets, to see signs advertising 'Bachelors for Rent' or even 'Large Bachelors' or 'Refinished Bachelors Available'!

MORTARBOARD

A literal mortarboard is a square board with a handle on the underside, used for holding mortar. The word 'mortar' itself comes from the Latin *mortarium,* meaning the round bowl in which drugs were mixed and pounded, and which, together with the pestle used for pounding, are now the symbol of the pharmaceutical profession. The bricklayer's cement would originally (in Roman times) have been mixed in a similar vessel, so it too came to be known as mortar.

The use of 'mortarboard' for the academic cap (because it looks like the bricklayer's tool upside down) started out as Victorian student slang. Our first quotation for it is from 1854, but it must have gained respectability fairly quickly, because by 1908 L.M. Montgomery was using it in *Anne of Green Gables* without quotation marks or any other indication that it wasn't standard vocabulary.

Before this, there were other words for academic caps. 'Cater-cap', derived from the French *quatre* because the cap has four corners, was in vogue between 1580 and 1700. 'Trencher cap' took over between 1700 and 1850. This was because the cap was seen as looking like a trencher, or slab of wood on which meat was served, with a basin sitting on it.

HERE COMES THE BRIDE

ॐ

Summer is also a popular time for weddings. Here we take you from the institution itself to the bride's undies, passing through parts of the wedding ceremony on the way.

WEDDING

'Wedding' goes all the way back to Old English: the verb 'wed' in Old English meant 'to pledge', and it could be any kind of pledging. For a while it was even used to mean 'wager or stake money', which may not seem so odd to those who think of marriage as a gamble. But even as early as Anglo-Saxon times it meant 'commit oneself to matrimony', and this is the only sense that has survived, other than the transferred sense, as in 'I'm not wedded to the idea', which has, surprisingly, been around since at least the 1500s.

WEDLOCK
Many people think 'wedlock' must have something to do with locks, because of the ending, but it doesn't. 'Wedlock' is derived from the Old English word *wed,* meaning a pledge, and the suffix *lác,* meaning 'the action of', and thus etymologically means 'the act of pledging'. If the suffix *lác* is related to any other Old English word at all, it is to one meaning 'play, fun, glee'. No balls and chains.

BRIDE, BRIDAL
'Bride' is yet another very old word. It goes back to the Anglo-Saxons, and it meant exactly then what it means now. 'Bridal', however, is interesting. It was originally a noun, literally meaning 'bride ale'. It used to mean the banquet and other festivities associated with the wedding, when, of course, the Anglo-Saxons would quaff a lot of ale. I guess wedding receptions haven't changed much in a thousand years. So 'bridal' was a noun for several centuries. But by about 1600 people started to think that it was an adjective meaning 'of a bride', because of that—*al* ending, as in words like 'nuptial' and 'mortal' and 'fatal', and they started using it as an adjective, hence our current usage, as in 'bridal party', 'bridal veil', and so on.

BRIDEGROOM
In Old English, the word was *brýdguma,* which came from *brýd,* meaning 'bride', plus *guma,* which was a poetic word for 'man'. But the word *guma* died out in the Middle Ages and by the 16th century people could no longer figure out why a man would be called a 'bridegoom'—not surprisingly. For a while in the 14th and 15th centuries, the word 'bride' applied to both sexes, so you

could have a male bride or a female bride, and perhaps with same-sex marriage this trend will be revived, who knows? In fact, a gay friend of mine who recently got married told me he and his partner had to decide which of them was going to be listed as the 'bride' on their marriage licence application! By Shakespeare's time, the word 'bridegoom' without an *r* was still sticking around, but people had reinvented the word as 'bridegroom', substituting the word 'groom', which in Old English had meant 'boy'. By the 1400s, 'groom' meant 'man', a 'fellow', just any sort of 'male person'. So that's how we ended up with 'bridegroom'.

Non-English speakers must often wonder why we use the same word for a husband on his wedding day that we use for someone who looks after horses. 'Groom' did not apply specifically to a servant looking after horses till some time later, in the 1600s. By the 1800s, the noun had become a verb as well (you see, it's not that shocking for nouns to do that), meaning 'care for horses'. The extended sense, meaning 'care for one's own appearance', dates from the late 19th century.

GOWN

In Late Latin, the word *gunna* meant 'fur', and by the 8th century the word was being used to mean a fur garment that elderly or sick monks were allowed to wear over their habits. This was borrowed into Old French as *goune*, a word that has completely died out in French but has survived in English after being borrowed in the 1300s. Originally, it meant any flowing garment worn by either sex; this has survived in the scholar's gown worn as part of academic dress. Until the 18th century 'gown' was the ordinary word for a women's garment, but it was then superseded by 'dress', leaving 'gown' to be used only for fancy dresses.

CORSAGE

Corsage was an Old French synonym for *cors* (modern French *corps*) meaning 'body', both words coming from the Latin *corpus*. It came into English in the 15th century. In 1658, we find the following statement: 'He thought the greatness of their stature and corsage would be a terrour to the Romans.' One has visions of an army transfixed by a gardenia. Gradually 'corsage' came to be restricted to mean a woman's upper body, then the bodice of a dress covering that part of the body, and finally the small bouquet worn on the bodice, often by the mothers of the bride and groom.

CUMMERBUND

This wide sash (often misspelled and mispronounced 'cumberbund' or 'cumberbun') is hardly ever seen these days except as part of the formal attire worn by grooms and their attendants. The word comes from the Urdu and Persian *kamar,* meaning 'loins', and *band,* meaning a tie or sash, so a cummerbund is literally a 'loin cloth'. No doubt that would turn heads if worn by a groom. The English borrowed it in the 1600s to mean a wide silk belt, presumably because this was a standard part of the attire worn by some Indians at the time.

USHER

An usher is not a person who ushes! The word is a corruption of the Old French *uissier* (modern French *huissier*), which in turn came from the classical Latin word for 'door', *ostium*. So an usher was originally someone who stood at a door and let people in. Gradually, ushers moved away from the door and showed people to their seats as well. *Ostium* hasn't given English or French any other words, because it wasn't in fact used much in the Latin that people spoke. In popular Latin the word for 'gate', *porta*, supplanted *ostium* as the word for 'door', which is why we instead have words like 'porter', 'portal', and 'porch' for things relating to doors.

AISLE

This word has an unnecessarily complicated spelling. Sometimes I think we should just revert to Middle English spellings; it would make our lives a lot easier. The word started out as the Latin word for 'wing', *ala*. In Old French this became *ele*. This came into English in the 1300s to mean one of the side parts of a church on either side of the nave, not just the part you walk along, but the whole side 'wing'. First of all, people confused 'ele' meaning 'wing' with 'ile' meaning 'island', thinking of it as a distinct part of the church. Now, 'ile' meaning island was spelled without an s in the Middle Ages. Then those Renaissance busybodies got a hold of it and said, 'Hey, it comes from Latin *insula*, so it should have an s in it!' (Thank God they didn't plump for the *n* as well!) So the 'ile' in a church started to be spelled 'isle' as well. Then in the 1700s people said, 'Wait a minute, the thing in the church doesn't come from *insula*, it comes from *ala* meaning wing, so we should put an *a* in it like in the French word for wing, *aile.*' So they crossed *aile* with *isle* and ended up with 'aisle', which is really quite ridiculous. And then, as if confusion wasn't rampant enough, the word got confused with 'alley', so that it ended up meaning the passageway between the seats in a church, not just the side parts of a church.

CONFETTI

This Italian word was derived from the Latin *confectus,* meaning 'prepared, pickled', which also gave us the old-fashioned English word 'comfit' for a candy. In fact, *confetti*, which in Italian is a plural noun, means 'candies', specifically those sugar-coated almonds that are given away at christenings and weddings and so on. It was the custom in Italy to throw these—or plaster imitations of them—during carnival time, at parades. The custom spread to southern France, particularly to Nice, in the mid-19th century, where people started thinking that maybe paper was better (and no doubt cheaper) to throw at people than plaster or hard almonds, and from there to England. 'Confetti' was originally a plural noun in English, becoming singular only in the 20th century.

BOMBONIERE

The Italian custom of giving sugared almonds at weddings has also given us the word 'bomboniere', small gifts traditionally accompanied by sugared almonds given to guests by the bride and groom. A number of Toronto florists and gift shops (including the intriguingly cross-cultural 'Hermes' House of Bomboniere' in Toronto's Greektown) sell these. The word (the singular is *bomboniera* and literally means 'candy dish' in Italian) was not entered in the first edition of the *Canadian Oxford Dictionary*, in spite of the fact that our Italian-Canadian lexicographer got married two years into the project, thus conveniently exposing us to real-world knowledge of the word and the thing. But it did receive an entry in the second edition of the dictionary, since we accumulated much more evidence of the word in use since then, including an item on the Home and Garden television network on how to make them yourself.

TROUSSEAU

I'm sure young brides admiring their lingerie don't think about this, but 'trousseau' and 'truss' are related! They both come ultimately from a vulgar Latin word *torsus,* meaning 'twisted'. In Old French, *torser* got switched around to *trousser,* meaning to bind up with string into a bundle. So a *trousse* was a bundle of some kind, especially the kind of pack you would load on the back of a donkey or horse. A *trousseau* was a smaller version of this, and already by the 1200s it was being used in French to mean the clothing and various objects given to a bride. We didn't borrow *trousseau* in this sense from French till the early 1800s, but we did borrow *trousse.* Now, if you think of the original pack-horse *trousse,* or truss, as being a pad fastened approximately to the loins of the animal with a belt, you can see why surgical trusses, which are mentioned as early as 1543, are called that, because they're basically a pad on a belt fastened around the loins.

There is a distinctly Canadian connection with the word 'trousseau'. This is the custom of the 'trousseau tea', a party hosted by a bride's mother for neighbours and acquaintances at which shower and wedding gifts, the bride's trousseau, and contents of her hope chest were displayed. The custom is now mostly extinct, but it was very much alive for women of my mother's generation and was uniquely Canadian.

EATING OUT ON CANADA DAY

৪১

The Canada Day weekend is usually a great opportunity for an outdoor feast, be it a picnic with its accoutrements and its uninvited six-legged guests, or a barbecue.

PICNIC

There is a folk etymology going around to the effect that 'picnic' is a racist term based on the lynching of blacks in 19th-century America. Some people even want the word banned because of this unfounded belief. But the first evidence for the word 'picnic' in English is from Lord Chesterfield's letters to his son in 1748, referring to a European custom which was essentially what we would now call a potluck dinner. It wasn't until about a century later that the outdoor element came to be important. For the first fifty years or so, all the references are to picnics in Germany or France rather than England. The word was in fact borrowed from French, where *pique-nique* has been recorded since 1692. These dates and the geography make any connection with lynching unlikely. In fact, *pique-nique* is derived from the verb *piquer*, which means 'to peck at', and *nique* which means 'something of little value', which in turn comes from a Germanic word, *nik*.

HAMPER

The word 'hamper' was originally 'hanaper', or the squished-down version 'hanper', which gives a rather difficult series of consonants to say, so 'hanper' became 'hamper'. A hanaper was a case to hold 'hanaps', which were drinking vessels or goblets. Originally this case could be made out of any substance, but by about 1500 wicker was most common, so gradually the idea arose that the defining element in 'hamper' was not what it contained but that it was made of wicker. So picnic baskets came to be known as hampers. The tradition of sending Christmas hampers (originally as gifts, now as a charitable undertaking) seems to have arisen in Victorian times.

JUNKET

While on the subject of picnics and baskets, I want to talk about 'junket', which started off meaning a basket. It comes from the

French word *jonc*, which means 'bulrush'. A *jonquette* in the Middle Ages was a basket woven from rushes, especially, for some reason, one used for catching or storing fish.

There is an old-fashioned dessert, sort of like sweetened cottage cheese, called junket. This is also related to the basket, because the milk and cream were left in the basket to turn into curds and drain. This was apparently a pretty fancy dessert in the 1500s, because soon 'junket' came to mean any dainty confection, and then a whole feast accompanied by much merrymaking. By the early 1800s it had come to mean an outing involving much eating and drinking, such as a picnic, and by the 1880s it was being used as it is now, to mean an all-expense-paid expedition, in which, it must be said, neither cottage cheese nor baskets made of bulrushes figure prominently.

BLANKET

'Blanket' comes from the French word *blanc*, meaning white; *blanquette* was originally a kind of white or undyed wool fabric. Very quickly the word came to apply to the large sheet of wool, of any colour, used to keep one warm in bed or to sit on for a picnic.

ANT

The word 'ant' started out in Old English as *amete*, and in some regions, Newfoundland being one, ants are still called 'emmets'. *Amete* got squished down to *amte*, which is hard to say, so the *m* got changed to an *n*, leaving us with 'ant'.

CRUMB

'Crumb' has meant a small piece of bread since Anglo-Saxon times, but the interesting question is, why is it spelled with a silent *b*? Until the 1500s, in fact, there was no *b*; the word was just 'crum' or 'cromme'. Even Samuel Johnson gives 'crum' as the first spelling. What happened was that 'crum' created a derivative, 'crummel', which then began to be pronounced 'crumble' by analogy with words like 'humble'. This was a very common phonetic transformation; it happened also with 'bramble' and 'mumble', among others. Then the derivative influenced the root word, at least in spelling, though never in pronunciation, until 'crumb' actually beat out 'crum', its final victory not happening till the 19th century.

BARBECUE

This word came into English from Spanish in the 1600s. The Spanish word was *barbacoa*, which the Spanish had picked up from the Arawak, a native people of the Caribbean. It originally meant a raised wooden platform of sticks for sleeping on, so our first evidence of the word is someone saying, 'We lay there all night on our barbecues.' A similar framework was also used to support meat above a fire for smoking or drying, which is clearly where the current sense of the word comes from. There is absolutely no truth to the rumour that this comes from the French 'barbe à queue', suggesting that an animal was roasted whole 'from its beard to its tail'.

SIRLOIN

A barbecue favourite is steak, about which word there is little to say: it comes from an Old Norse word which is related to a word meaning 'roast on a spit'. The type of steak called 'sirloin' is more interesting. There is no truth to the myth (circulating since at least the 1600s) that the sirloin is so called because it was 'knighted' by an English king and thus, from being an ordinary loin, became 'Sir Loin'. It is simply an English corruption of the French word *surlonge*, meaning 'on or above the loin', because it is the upper part of the loin. For a long time it was spelled 'surloin' in English, but the *sir* spelling won out, probably as a result of the popularity of the folk etymology.

MARINADE

One of the secrets to great barbecued meat is the marinade. The ultimate origin of this word is the word 'marine', because originally a marinade was simply salt water in which meat or fish were pickled or preserved. Usually there was no further cooking after the marinade stage, so you just took your pilchard and put it in salt water, and ate it after that. Sounds disgusting. Maybe it *was* disgusting, so people started adding other ingredients to the marinade, such as wine and flavourings. Gradually the primary purpose of a marinade ceased being pickling or preserving, and came to be adding flavour and tenderizing.

APRON

'Apron' is one of the most fascinating words in the English language. It is, surprisingly, related to both 'napkin' and 'map'. They all have their roots in the Latin word *mappa*, which meant a table napkin or tablecloth. When this migrated into French, the *m* was transformed into an *n*, leaving us with the modern French words *nappe* (a tablecloth) and *napperon* (originally a small tablecloth, now a placemat). The English took the word *nappe* and added their diminutive suffix '-kin' to give us 'napkin'. What happened to *napperon* was a little more unusual. In the 1300s and 1400s, people in England talked about 'naprons', as in 'she was wearing her napron' (pronounced NAPPrun). But by the late 1400s people had become confused, thinking 'a napron' was 'an apron', so the *n* at the beginning got dropped. And then, because of the Great Vowel Shift, the pronunciation APPrun changed to EHprun.

But what has this got to do with maps? Well, in medieval Latin, two-dimensional representations of the world were called a *mappa mundi*, literally the 'tablecloth of the world', because they were shaped like a tablecloth and presumably spread out over a table to look at. Eventually the name 'map' stuck for cartographic purposes.

BUCCANEER

Finally, a word that you would never suspect had anything to do with barbecues, but it does! When the French arrived in the Caribbean in the 1600s they encountered a native word which they interpreted as *boucan*, meaning, essentially, a barbecue in the sense of a frame on which to smoke or cook meat. To this day in Canadian French, the word *boucane* is a synonym of the European French word for smoke, *fumée*. A *boucanier* was originally some-one who dried or smoked the meat of wild oxen or boars on one of these frames. Since this wasn't much of a livelihood, they had to find some way of supplementing their income. Apparently, the easiest way to do this was to set up as a pirate and raid the wealthy Spanish colonies around the Caribbean. And thus 'buccaneer' came to mean a pirate.

THE DOG DAYS OF SUMMER

ॐ

By late July, we are at the height of summer. Why do we call them 'the dog days of summer'? For that matter, where do the word 'dog' and names for various dogs come from? And why is there a plant with a name that sounds as though it should be a dog?

DOG DAYS

The expression 'dog days' has its origin in astronomy. The bright-est star in the night sky is Sirius, a name which means 'sparkling' or 'scorching' in Greek. Sirius is also known as the Dog Star, because it is the chief star in the constellation Canis major or 'The Greater Dog', which the Greeks fancifully conceived of as one of the dogs following the hunter Orion. Sirius passes through a period when it is not visible because it rises and sets during daylight. But at a certain point during the summer, it becomes visible again just before sunrise. This reappearance (usually sometime in July) coincides with the hottest part of the year, and it was the ancient Romans who made the connection between the star and the weather, calling the forty days following its appearance the 'dog days' or 'canicular days' (from *canis*, the Latin word for 'dog').

The Dog Star suffered from a bad rap; the Egyptians believed that its rising caused the Nile to flood, and the Romans blamed it for all sorts of pernicious things as well as the unbearable heat. It was generally believed also that it caused dogs to go mad, and as late as the 16th century people were even advised not to have sex during the dog days! In English, this benighted time of year was first known as the 'canicular days', about 1400, and even today in French the word for 'heat wave' is *canicule*. The simpler 'dog days' doesn't show up until 1538.

DOG, HOUND
The generic name for a canine in Old English was not 'dog', but 'hound' (it would have been pronounced HOOND back then). This has cognates in all Germanic languages, notably modern German, where the word for 'dog' is *Hund*. But then, just before the Norman Conquest, the word 'dog' cropped up in English, and no one knows why or where it came from. Originally it seems to have been applied to a particular breed of hound noted for its strength, but soon it spread to all domestic canines and took over from 'hound'.

PUPPY
This comes to us from the French word *poupée* meaning 'doll', which in turn comes from popular Latin *puppa*, which meant a young girl. The same French and Latin roots have also given us the word 'puppet', and for a while in the 1600s 'puppet' was also used to mean a young dog. But 'puppy' has been around longer. When

it entered English in the 1400s, it meant not so much a young dog as a very small dog (especially a woman's lap dog), what is often called a 'toy dog', hence the connection between dolls and dogs. Shakespeare provides the first evidence we have for 'puppy' meaning a young dog. Now, of course, there was a word to designate that creature before Shakespeare: the very old word, dating back to Anglo-Saxon times, 'whelp'. But this word has lost out to the upstart 'puppy'. The contemptuous use of 'puppy' to apply to a person (in its modern manifestation 'a sick puppy') is of about the same vintage (late 1500s) as the 'dog' sense.

SPANIEL

Spaniels were originally a Spanish breed, so in Old French their name was *ménagier espaignol*, which means 'Spanish dog'. The noun meaning 'dog' was dropped, and the adjective alone was borrowed into English at about Chaucer's time as 'spaynyell', which gradually became 'spaniel'. A cocker spaniel is so called because the breed was originally trained to scare up woodcocks and other birds for hunters.

POODLE

'Poodle' comes from German *Pudelhund*, literally 'puddle dog', because poodles were developed as water retrievers (the custom of clipping their coats came about to make it easier for them to manoeuvre in water).

GREYHOUND

Greyhounds are not necessarily grey, so why are they called this? Dogs of this type were already being called *grighund* in about 1000. The first element is actually a corruption of an Old English word *gri*, which meant 'female dog'. This lost out to 'bitch' (also an Old English word). So by 1600, people didn't know what the original 'gri' meant and confused it with the word 'grey'.

HOREHOUND

Horehound is not, as you might think, a type of dog with loose morals even by canine standards, but a plant of the mint family. Its extract has traditionally been used in cough remedies. The word dates back to Old English times, when it was *hárhúne*, literally 'a hoary plant'. *Hár* meant 'grey-haired with age' and survives also in 'hoarfrost' and 'hoary'. The plant was called this because its stem and leaves are covered with a white cottony substance. By the 1400s, *húne*, which had dropped out of the language, became confused with 'hound' (which as we have seen, rhymed with MOONED before the Great Vowel Shift).

Preserving Summer's Bounty

❧

July and August are busy months for the home canner as various fruits come into season, just begging to be turned into delectable preserves. Being an avid jam maker myself, I can only agree with this quotation from the Duke of Newcastle in 1676: 'What an admirable thing it is for a Lady...to be skilfull in the great secret of Preserving, making Marmalads, Quidenies [a quince jam] and Gellies.'

JAM

'Jam' is a bit of a mystery. It cropped up in about the 1700s. An early English lexicographer, Nathan Bailey, who seems to have been surprisingly good at folk etymology, suggested it came from the French *j'aime*, meaning 'I like', the theory being that French kids would eat jam and say, '*J'aime*'! Twenty years later, Samuel Johnson was much more frank. His entry for the word says '**Jam** (I know not whence derived) a conserve of fruits boiled with sugar water'.

I wish I could get away with doing that in my dictionaries. People are always saying we should be more like Samuel Johnson! But the most likely explanation is that the noun 'jam' is related to the verb 'jam', which arose about the same time (around 1700) to mean 'press or squeeze tightly between two objects'. This may in turn be a corruption of 'champ' (in the 'crush with one's teeth' sense).

JELLY
This was borrowed in the Middle Ages from the French word for frost, gelée, which in turn came from the Latin gelata, meaning 'frozen or congealed'. A jelly in English was originally the congealed savoury dish that we would now call an aspic, made from boiling down the gelatinous parts of animals.

MARMALADE
Marmalade was originally a solid jelly dessert made of quinces, rather than a citrus fruit jam as we now know it. The word came into English in the late 15th century from Portuguese, the word for quince in Portuguese being marmelo. The Portuguese word came ultimately from Greek melimelon, literally 'honey apple', applied to a kind of apple grafted on a quince tree.

There is a folk etymology about 'marmalade'. The story goes that Mary Queen of Scots fell ill and was served this delectable dessert to fortify her, as a result it was dubbed 'Marie malade' or 'sick Mary'. The less said about this folk etymology the better!

SYRUP
Syrup is the essential medium for canning fruit. The word comes ultimately from the Arabic word sharab, meaning 'wine' or some other drink. Sharab in turn comes from the word shurb, which meant 'drink' and which also turns up in 'sherbet' and in 'shrub', not the small tree but a now-obsolete drink made from rum, sugar, and orange or lemon juice, or from a raspberry syrup. Our

earliest evidence of the word 'syrup' in English is from the 1390s and shows that syrups were used for both medicinal and culinary purposes even then.

PEACH

Peaches were originally cultivated in China about 2000 BC. They migrated westward until they reached Greece at about 300 BC from Persia. Because of their perceived Persian origin, the Romans called the peach a 'Persian apple', or *persicum malum*. In time this was shortened to *persica*. As it passed into French, *persica* got squished down to *persca*, then to *pesca*, and finally to *pêche*, which is the word the English borrowed at about Chaucer's time. They don't seem to have had peaches in England before then.

CHERRY

'Cherry' comes from a popular Latin word *ceresea*, which became the French word for the fruit, *cerise*, or in the Northern French dialect, *cherise*. So the question is, why is there an *s* on the end of this word in French and not in English? Well, there *was* an *s* at the end of the English word when we first borrowed it from the French. You would have one *cherise* and many *cherises*. But this was too much for the English speakers, for whom an –*s* ending suggested a plural, so they dropped the *s* in the singular and made it 'cherry'.

The same thing happened with peas. Before 1600, the word for a singular pea was 'pease', as in the nursery rhyme 'Pease porridge hot, pease porridge cold, pease porridge in the pot nine days old'. Again people got confused and dropped the *s* for the singular. This phenomenon is still alive and well. Consider the number of people who use 'gladiola' as the 'singular' of 'gladiolus'. Likewise, one day someone walked past my front garden, where I have a multitude of cosmos flowers growing, and told me that if it were up to her, she would pull up every last 'cosmo' from her garden. Similarly, a local flower shop where the owners are Chinese-speakers was advertising amaryllis as 'ama lilies'. The phenomenon is not limited to plants. Recently a new 'singular' for the large muscles in the thighs and arms has been created. Thus people refer to their 'tricep', 'bicep', and 'quadricep' muscles, though the correct singulars are 'triceps', 'biceps', and 'quadriceps'. In fact, as I wrote that last sentence, my spellchecker complained about 'tricep' and 'quadricep' (it even automatically corrected the latter to 'quadriceps'), but it was quite happy with 'bicep'.

GRAPE

'Grape' started out meaning not the individual fruit but the bunch. In Old French, as indeed in modern French, the singular *raisin* is the word for grapes collectively, and a *grappe de raisin* is a bunch of grapes. *Grappe* came into French from Germanic, where it meant a hook (the same word has also given us 'grapple'). The theory is that grapes were gathered with a vine hook and therefore a *grappe* was the quantity that you would get with your hook. Now, the Anglo-Saxons hadn't had much to do with grapes before the French arrived, so they were a bit mystified by this *grappe de raisin* business and immediately took *grappe* to mean the individual fruit. But they didn't leave *raisin* by the wayside. French uses the same word *raisin* whether the fruit is fresh or dried. The English loved adopting French words if it allowed them to make a semantic distinction (as they had done to distinguish 'veal' from 'calf'). So Middle English speakers held on to 'raisin' for the dried grapes.

APRICOT

We acquired this word from the Spanish or Portuguese in the 1550s. Their word was *albricoque*, which they had got from the Arabs in the Iberian Peninsula, *al* meaning 'the' and *barquq* being an Arabic corruption of the Latin *praecocia* meaning 'ripening early', which has also given us the word precocious'. *Praecocia* came from *prae-* meaning 'before' and *coquere* meaning to cook or to ripen, and literally meant 'to boil beforehand'. Now 'albricock', as the English first spelled it, got changed to 'apricot' under the belief that it was derived from another Latin phrase, *aprico coctus*, which would have meant 'ripened in a sunny place', and indeed would have been applicable to this and all fruit.

CURRANT
There are two quite separate items of food called currants. The first are the small black dried fruits used in scones and fruitcakes. These are actually a type of raisin. The other currants are a type of berry, which come in two varieties, redcurrants and blackcurrants.

The currants found in scones come from a small black grape that was originally grown in Corinth in Greece. As a result they were called 'raisins of Corinth', and indeed to this day are called *raisins de Corinthe* in French. In the Anglo-French dialect that was spoken in England in the Middle Ages, this came out as 'raisins de Corauntz', which got changed to 'raisins of currants', until people finally thought 'currants' was just the word designating that fruit. Because it appeared to be plural to boot—that s on the end—they had to invent a singular, 'currant'.

Then, in the 1500s, the berries we know as redcurrants and blackcurrants were introduced into England from Northern Europe, and people thought they were the fresh variety of the dried currant and started using the same name for them.

MELON
This is a contraction of two Greek words, *melon* meaning 'apple' and *pepon* meaning 'gourd'. *Melopepon* was a bit of a mouthful, so it got shortened quite quickly, even before it passed into French from Latin. But literally, a melon is an 'apple gourd'.

CANTALOUPE
This melon is named after Cantalupo, the name of a former coun-

try seat of the Pope near Rome, where the melons were said to have been first cultivated after being introduced from Armenia.

RHUBARB
Rhubarb was a plant foreign to Europe, and was originally imported from the Far East by way of Russia. The Greeks called it *rha*, which may have been an old name for the Volga River. The Romans insisted even more on the foreignness of it by tacking on the adjective *barbarum* meaning 'foreign', to give *rhabarbarum*. *Barbarum* has also given us 'barbarian', 'barbarous', and even 'Barbary'. It came from an imitative Greek word meaning 'babbling'. To the ancient Greeks, people speaking foreign languages sounded as if they were babbling, so the Greeks called all foreigners *barbaros*. The Greeks naturally thought that anyone who didn't have the good fortune to be Greek was automatically uncivilized, and this is how 'barbarian' came to mean 'uncivilized'. Although rhubarb was introduced to England in the 1400s, it wasn't until the late 1800s that people realized the stems could be eaten.

Hitting the Road

ॐ

The August long weekend observed in most parts of Canada is a good time to start out on a road trip and to think about car-related words.

ROAD
The meaning that we most commonly associate with the word 'road', that is, 'a way with a prepared surface for vehicles and pedestrians to travel on', is surprisingly recent. Our first evidence

of this meaning is in Shakespeare, so around 1600.

But other meanings of the word have been around much longer. 'Road' is related to the verb 'to ride' and originally (in Alfred the Great's time) meant 'a journey on horseback', and more specifically 'a foray by mounted men against an enemy'. This particular sense was also the origin of 'inroad', which originally meant a hostile incursion (where people 'rode in' to enemy territory), before it took on the figurative sense of an encroachment that survives in the expression 'make inroads'.

Incidentally, a Scottish variation of 'road' meaning one of these mounted expeditions was 'raid'. The Old English form was *rade* (pronounced RAHduh), and even back then the Scots pronounced things differently. Interestingly, this word was alive in Scottish English in the 1400s and 1500s, then died out completely until the 19th century when it was revived by Sir Walter Scott. So it is thanks to him that we have the word 'raid' (he also revived its synonym 'foray'), and of course in the 20th century it got adapted for other kinds of attacks, so we have air raids and so on.

A sense of 'road' that is earlier than the common 'passage for vehicles' is 'a sheltered piece of water near the shore where vessels lie at anchor in safety'—where they may, so to speak, 'ride upon the waves'. This dates back to the 1300s and survives in Canada in the name of 'Royal Roads', the former military college near Victoria, which some people may have always thought was an unusual name for a naval academy!

ROUTE

So, one may wonder, what on earth did people call a passage for vehicles before 1596 if they didn't call it a road? Well, 'route' had a certain vogue from about 1200 on. This was borrowed from French, which got it from the late popular Latin *rupta,* meaning 'broken', the theory being that there was a word *rupta via,* meaning 'broken path', just as we would talk about 'breaking a trail'.

WAY

But even older than 'route' is 'way', which was the Old English word for a path, track, or road, and even meant a main road. This now survives in proper names such as Kingsway and Queensway.

HIGHWAY

This brings us to 'highway', which amazingly is very, very old; in fact, it first turns up in 859. (We can assume that they were somewhat different back then!) 'High' in this word did not mean 'elevated or tall'. Rather, it meant 'of great importance', a meaning that has survived in only a few other compounds in modern English, for example 'high altar', 'high mass', 'high days and holy days', and in British English, 'High Street'.

STREET

'Street' is another very old word. It comes from Latin *via strata*, meaning 'paved way', abbreviated to *strata*. Unlike most Latin-derived words, which came into English either through the Church or through Old French after the Norman Conquest, or even later, post-Renaissance, directly from Latin, this word had already been borrowed from the Romans by the Germanic tribes before they even left the continent for England. The Romans were great road builders, and there was much contact between Germanic peoples and the Romans, both within the empire and on its fringes. Obviously the Germanic peoples would have been impressed with these amazing 'streets' and borrowed the word to describe them. Then when they got to England, they met the native Celts who had also almost certainly borrowed the word from Latin, since the Romans had, after all, occupied Britain (building roads frantically the while) from 43 AD to the mid-400s.

GAS

Very unusually, we know exactly when this word was invented. It was 1652, and the inventor was a Dutch chemist by the name of J.B. van Helmont, who had a theory that all bodies contained a substance not readily detected, which he thought was water in a state as lacking in density as possible. He took the Greek word *khaos*, which is the root of 'chaos', and Dutchified it into the word 'gas'. His theory was disproved, but a century or so later, when people started to understand gaseous states, his word stuck.

When gasoline was invented in the mid-1800s, its name was created from 'gas' (presumably because it was so volatile), '-ol' from 'alcohol', and '-ine', which is used in names of chemical derivatives. Gasoline got shortened back to 'gas' again very quickly: we have a quotation from an advertisement in a 1911 *Victoria Daily Colonist*: 'Having installed a new portable gasoline wagon, we can supply you with "gas" in record time from our central garage.'

OIL, PETROLEUM

'Oil' comes to us ultimately from the Latin word for 'olive', *olea*. *Oleum* was olive oil, and by extension any substance similar to it. 'Petroleum' comes from *oleum* combined with *petrus* meaning rock; it is an oil that comes from rocks.

FUEL

If you look at the word 'fuel', it looks like a dyslexic version of the French word *feu,* meaning fire. And indeed this is where we got 'fuel' from: it was originally *feuaile* in Middle English. The French got *feuaile* from doing their usual consonant-dropping on a Latin word, in this case the word *focalia,* meaning roughly 'something to feed a fire', which derived from the word for 'fire', which was *focus*.

So if *focus* meant 'fire', one wonders, how did it come to mean what it does today in English? Well, this we owe to Johannes Kepler, the German astronomer, who first used 'focus' in the sense of the point to which lines converge in 1604. When you think of that old science experiment of using a magnifying glass to set fire to a piece of paper, you realize that the 'focus' is in fact the 'fire point'.

TIRE

Tires have, surprisingly, been with us since the late 1400s. Back then, if you went shopping at Ye Olde Canadian Tire, what you got was a set of curved pieces of iron plate to cover your wooden carriage wheels. Not very shock-absorbing! The word was a shortening of 'attire': tires were what you 'clothed' your wheels with. 'Attire' came from a French word, *atirier*, which meant 'to arrange in a row'. It is related to our word 'tier' as in 'tiers of seats', and also, more surprisingly, to the word 'artillery'. The *artillerie* in 13th-century France was all of your weapons of war lined up in a row; it got narrowed down to cannon and guns in the 14th century.

The people we have to thank for the nice shock-absorbing tires on our vehicles instead of iron plates are cyclists (long may we rule!). Pneumatic tires were invented by Robert Thomson in 1845, but they didn't catch on because people preferred solid rubber tires, probably thinking they were more durable. But then cycling started to take off, and in 1888, John Dunlop, a Belfast veterinarian, revived the idea of air-filled rubber tires and patented them for bicycles. Then the Michelin company in France adapted pneumatic tires for cars in 1895.

That's the story on tires, and I think it's just as well that 'attire' got shortened to 'tire', because shopping at the 'Canadian Attire' store would be way too confusing.

DASHBOARD

A dashboard was originally a board or wide strip of leather across the front of a cart or carriage to prevent mud from being splashed by the heels of the horses into the interior—to prevent the occupants from being 'dashed' with mud. Dashboards for horse-drawn carriages seem to have been invented in the mid-1800s, and already by 1874 the word had been shortened to 'dash'. When automobiles were invented, the instrument panel, which was in an analogous position, was called a dashboard or dash almost immediately.

PARK

'Park' was a word we got from the Normans to designate an enclosed tract of land for keeping and hunting deer and other game. This in turn may have come from a post-classical Latin word, *parricus*, meaning 'fence'. Gradually the word came to apply to all sorts of enclosed areas of land reserved for a certain purpose, including, in the 1600s, an area used for storing the artillery and vehicles of a military expedition. So placing or leaving your cannon and wagons in one of these enclosures came to be known as 'parking' them. By the mid-1800s this had spread from military slang to general usage for all sorts of vehicles.

NEGOTIATE

This will come as no surprise to people who sit around the bargaining table till the wee hours, but 'negotiate' literally means 'no leisure'. It comes from the Latin negative prefix *neg-* and *otium* meaning 'leisure'. *Negotium* in Latin meant a business occupation. This idea still survives in French, where the word *négociant* means a dealer or trader. You can see how arranging a business transaction can involve conferring until a mutually beneficial arrangement has been reached, but in English the commercial connotations of 'negotiate' have never been strong; they've been overshadowed by the idea of discussion to reach a settlement or compromise. Indeed, the idea of overcoming difficulties on the way to a goal is so strong that we can now negotiate bends in the road, something we would often have to do on a road trip.

TENNIS, ANYONE?

ॐ

Mid-August brings with it the Canadian open tennis championships.

TENNIS

The word 'tennis' is older than you might think. The game of batting a ball around a court seems to have been brought to England by the French in the 1300s. The French apparently yelled out, '*Tenez*' before they served, *tenez* being a form of the French verb meaning 'to hold', used as an interjection meaning 'Here, take it'. So in effect they were saying, 'Take this, you guy on the other side!'

This got Anglicized into teNETZ, then teNESS, until finally the accent shifted and we ended up with 'tennis'. From 1400 to the late 1800s, tennis was played indoors, what we now call 'court tennis' and the English call 'real tennis'. Then in 1873 a Major Walter Wingfield invented a version of the game played outdoors on a lawn. But he decided to be clever and make up a Greek name for it, 'sphairistike', pronounced sfairISStickee. This purportedly meant 'the art of ball-playing'. (He did, however, offer 'lawn tennis' as an alternative.) Not surprisingly, 'sphaırıstıke' did not catch on, partly because people insisted on mispronouncing it to rhyme with 'spike'. There was even a snappy short form, 'stické', but that didn't catch on either. Thank God; otherwise we'd have to talk about the Canadian open stické championships. Inevitably, the name 'lawn tennis' won out. As this became the most common form of tennis, and partly because it wasn't always played on lawns, it was shortened to simply 'tennis'. And then, ironically, the French borrowed it back from English as *le tennis*.

RACQUET

'Racquet' comes ultimately from an Arabic word, *rahet*, which meant the palm of the hand. This got transferred into French through medieval Latin as *rachete* in the 1300s. Back then, in the form of tennis being played by the French, the ball was batted around with the palm of the hand. In fact, in French the game was called *jeu de paume*, or ('game of the palm'), which may be familiar as the name of a museum in Paris, or as a decisive event at the beginning of the French Revolution called the Tennis Court Oath. By 1500, however, when the English borrowed the French word, now spelled *raquette*, I guess people had got fed up with having their hands bruised to a pulp and were already using the stringed bat.

SEED

The notion of 'seeding' in tennis was invented in the 1890s in the United States. By sprinkling the top-ranked players throughout the competition, much as you would scatter seeds on a field, you ensured that the best players didn't compete against each other until the later stages of the tournament.

LOVE

By the 1600s, the practice of playing a game just for fun, without keeping score, was known as playing 'for love'. From there, 'love' came to mean 'no score' in games such as whist and tennis. There is no truth to the folk etymology that this comes from the French word *l'oeuf* meaning 'the egg', with the explanation being that eggs are ovoid and so are zeroes.

LET

'Let' in the tennis sense comes from a very old Anglo-Saxon word meaning to hinder or delay. So 'let him sing' meant 'prevent him from singing'. Meanwhile, the other 'let', which started out in

Anglo-Saxon meaning 'leave behind', gradually came to mean 'allow'. It was too hard on everyone's brains to have two 'let's' which meant completely opposite things. 'Let him sing': are we allowing him to sing or preventing him from singing? So the 'hindrance' let died out of the language, surviving only in the rather literary phrase 'without let or hindrance' and in tennis, where it designates the obstruction of the ball in some way, usually by hitting the net.

STORMY WEATHER

Summer brings its share of violent weather. Even hurricanes are known to visit Eastern Canada towards the end of August and beginning of September.

HURRICANE

'Hurricane' comes, not surprisingly, from a Caribbean language, Taino, which was spoken in the Bahamas and Greater Antilles but is now extinct. In Taino, *hurakán* meant 'god of the storm'. In the 1500s, when Europeans started exploring the Caribbean and having their first taste of violent tropical storms, they adapted this native word: the Spanish as *huracán* and the Portuguese as *furacão*. The English in turn borrowed the word from them and, for the first hundred or so years, the word in English was more commonly 'furicano' or 'furacane'. There were about thirty different spellings until it finally settled down as 'hurricane' in about 1680. Incidentally, from about 1750 to 1800, the word 'hurricane' was also used to mean a kind of fashionable social gathering, especially one where your house was overrun with people. For example, a quotation from 1746 reads: 'A confused meeting of company of both sexes on Sundays is called a hurricane.'

TYPHOON

A typhoon and a hurricane are technically the same thing, just occurring in different parts of the world. The word 'typhoon' is exceedingly cross-cultural. When English-speakers first encountered these storms in India in the 1500s, they naturally borrowed the Urdu word for the phenomenon, *tufan*. And for about 300 years, the British in India called these storms 'touffans'. Meanwhile, however, there was also a Chinese word for this type of storm, *tai fung,* which meant literally 'big wind'. People who had more contact with China than with India tended to use this word, or something like it. As luck would have it, the ancient Greek word for 'whirlwind' was *tuphon*. In the 1500s, people tended to think that all words had to come from Greek or Latin, so they messed around with these Urdu and Chinese words to make them look more like the Greek word until we finally ended up with 'typhoon' in the 19th century.

MONSOON

'Monsoon' came into English from Portuguese in about 1600. The Portuguese were exploring the Far East at the time, stocking up on exotic goods. They had got the word from Arabic, where *mawsim* means 'season' or 'seasonal wind'.

TORNADO

Tornadoes were originally just very violent thunderstorms on the tropical Atlantic, not necessarily accompanied by twisting funnel clouds. In fact, the original word in Spanish was *tronada*, which meant 'thunderstorm'. But as the word came to be applied to twisting wind storms, *tronada* got confused with another Spanish word, *tornado*, which means 'turned'.

CLOUD

'Cloud' is one of those words that you would bet goes back to Anglo-Saxon times. And indeed it does, to the Old English *clúd*, only back then it didn't mean the puffy things up in the sky but rather a mass of rock or a hill. It would have been pronounced KLOOD, and was related to the word that has given us a clod of earth.

So the question is, if the Anglo-Saxons didn't use *clúd* to mean the things in the sky, what did they call them? Their word was 'welkin', which I think we should revive, because it would be great to hear 'variable welkiness' in a forecast. But 'welkin' was doomed to failure.

First of all, in about 1200, it got bumped by a Norse newcomer, *sky*, which the Vikings had brought with them when they invaded the North of England (as we have already seen, most words beginning with *sk-* in English are of Norse origin). 'Sky' originally meant 'cloud' before it meant what we understand by 'sky'. Until then, 'heaven' had been the word for the blue stuff up there, so you had 'skies in the heaven', not 'clouds in the sky'. But already by about 1300 'sky' was beginning to mean the thing containing the clouds rather than the clouds themselves (although, considering the weather in Britain, it's often hard to distinguish the two!). So again, English needed a word for the puffy things, and this time it took the word that meant a hill or clump of earth and applied it to the meteorological phenomenon (because I guess if you look at clouds from a distance they look kind of like hills off on the horizon).

RAIN CATS AND DOGS

No one really knows where 'rain cats and dogs' comes from. The enmity of cats and dogs has been proverbial since at least the 1500s, and this idea of violence that's attached to cats and dogs may have been transferred so it could just mean 'rain violently'.

There are many folk etymologies for the phrase, all of them implausible:

- In Norse mythology, cats were supposed to have an influence on the weather. Witches that rode on storms were supposed to be accompanied by cats, so there's this idea that there's a connection between cats and wind and rain. Dogs were associated with the wind. Dogs and wolves were attendants of Odin, who was the storm god. So as a result of all of this, maybe cats were a symbol of rain, and dogs were a symbol of gusts of wind.
- It comes from the mass drowning of cats and dogs in heavy rainstorms in London; their corpses washed up in the gutters as if they had fallen from the sky. It would have to be a pretty torrential downpour for cats and dogs to drown!
- Cats and dogs lived in the thatched roofs of houses in Elizabethan times; when it rained, the roof became slippery so they would fall off the roof as if they were falling from the sky. Considering how much it rains in England, you would think that the cats and dogs would learn pretty quickly not to hang around on rain-soaked roofs, even supposing they lived there in the first place!

HARD TO KEEP THEM DOWN ON THE FARM

❧

Summer is the time for agricultural fairs, the biggest one being the Canadian National Exhibition ('exhibition' in this sense being a Canadianism) in Toronto at the end of August. Here are some words you probably never suspected had something to do with farming originally.

BORDELLO

This word was borrowed from Italian in the 1500s, though there was a much earlier form, 'bordel', borrowed from Old French in the 1200s. Originally, in French, a *bordel* or *borde* was a small farm or cottage, either because it was literally a hut made of boards, or because it was perceived as being on the borders or edges of civilization. There's no historical explanation for its leap from the farm to its current meaning, but I'll leave that to your imagination.

VERSE

In Latin the word for 'turn' was *versus*. Specifically the word was used for the turn made by a plough at the edge of a field. You got to the end of your furrow, then you turned around and went back the other way. This was extended to mean a line of writing, because of the similarity in appearance between lines of writing and furrows in a ploughed field. So very early on in English, back in Anglo-Saxon times, the word was borrowed from Latin to mean a single line of poetry. It wasn't until the 14th century that it came to apply to a whole stanza of poetry and to poetry itself.

REHEARSE

The ancient Romans had a farm implement that looked like a large rake which they used as a harrow to break up clods of earth and cover seeds. This was called a *hirpex*, a word that the Romans had got in their turn from the word for 'wolf' in the language of their ancient neighbours the Samnites; the rake was supposed to look like the wolf's teeth! In Old French, the Latin word got squished down to *herce,* and the French also created a verb *hercer* meaning 'to harrow', and *rehercer* to re-harrow, or, figuratively, to go over again, to repeat. When *rehercer* was borrowed into English in the 1300s it didn't mean 'practise for a theatrical performance' but simply 'repeat aloud'. It wasn't until Shakespeare's time that the theatrical sense developed.

HEARSE

Because the meanings of 'hearse' and 'rehearse' are so different, you would never suspect that they came from the same source, even though they look so much alike. But 'hearse', too, comes from the Latin *hirpex*. In addition to designating a harrow, the French word *herce* was also borrowed into medieval English to mean an elaborate framework, similar in shape to a harrow, carrying a large number of lighted candles that was placed over the coffin during funerals. By Shakespeare's time the word had come to mean the coffin itself and by the mid-1600s a carriage for transporting a coffin.

TRIBULATION

The Ancient Romans had a device for threshing grain called a *tribulum*, which consisted of a board with sharp points on the underside. This came from the verb *terere* meaning 'to rub'. From the name of the threshing tool, the Romans derived, not surprisingly, a verb meaning 'oppress or afflict', *tribulare*, and this has given us the word tribulation.

TOIL

The Romans also had a machine for crushing olives, called a *tudicula*, derived from a verb meaning 'to crush'. From this word they derived the word *tudiculare,* meaning to stir about or mix up. *Tudiculare* was borrowed into Old French and squished down to *toiler*. For the French it meant specifically to be embroiled or mixed up in a dispute or battle. When the word came into English in the 1300s, it meant to be engaged, not so much in physical, bloody battle, but in a legal battle; there was a strong sense of legal dispute or argument. It was only about a hundred years later that 'toil' came to mean arduous labour.

TOILET

'Toil' and 'toilet', perhaps surprisingly, are totally unrelated. But the word 'toilet' is so fascinating that it would be a shame not to look at it here, even though it has nothing to do with farming! It is related to the French word *toilette*, which literally means a little *toile*, *toile* meaning 'cloth' in French, coming ultimately from the Latin *tela* meaning web. And indeed, when the word 'toilet' was first used in English, in the 1500s, it meant a small piece of cloth, like a shawl, especially when this was used to protect clothing during a haircut. Already we see the connection with, shall we say, personal grooming. From there, the word went through a number of interesting phases: it meant a cloth cover for a dressing table, the items placed on such a cloth and used for personal grooming (for example, brushes, combs, mirrors), and then the table itself. This gave rise to some quotations that in retrospect are hilarious, such as Edward Gibbon saying of his *Decline and Fall of the Roman Empire*: 'My book was on every table, and almost on every toilet'! It became very fashionable in the 1700s for a woman to receive visitors as she was concluding her morning ablutions. Because it was common to describe a woman as being 'at her toilet' meaning 'at her dressing table', people came to understand 'at her toilet' as meaning 'in the process of washing, grooming, and dressing'. By the early 1800s, the word had come to mean an entire dressing room, especially one with washing facilities, and eventually, by the late 1800s, to the specific plumbing fixture itself or the room in which one is enclosed.

FORE!

ॐ

The first week of September brings us the Canadian open golf championships.

GOLF

It is uncertain where this word comes from. But it definitely does not come from the acronym for 'Gentlemen Only Ladies Forbidden', as one folk etymology alleges. There is a Dutch word *kolf*, which means 'a club or bat used in various games', but the word 'golf' is found in Scottish English long before any of these Dutch sports existed. The first references to golf come from the 1400s, in laws attempting to ban the sport because it interfered with the practice of archery, which was necessary for defending the nation. Rather morbidly, our first mention of golf clubs is from 1508, in an account of a criminal trial where one was used as a murder weapon!

PUTT

This came about simply as a result of the Scottish pronunciation of the verb 'put', especially in the sense of throwing a ball, as in 'shotput'. The Scots pronounced 'put' as 'putt', and since golf is originally a Scottish game, the pronunciation was adopted outside Scots English for this one usage.

LINKS

Golf links have no connection with the word 'link' meaning 'connect'. 'Links' comes from an Old English word, *hlinc*, meaning rising ground or a ridge. In southern England this word died out, but it survived in Scotland meaning 'gently rolling sandy ground covered with grass near the sea shore'. These were probably the original golf courses.

HAZARD

Hazard was originally, in the Middle Ages, a gambling game using two dice, in which the chances of winning were complicated by a set of arbitrary rules. The English got it from the French and the French got it from the Spanish who had got it from the Arabs, who occupied Spain throughout much of the Middle Ages. In Arabic, *al-zahr* means chance or luck; it seems to come from a Persian or Turkish word meaning 'dice'. It wasn't surprising that the name of the game came to be used to mean 'risk' and specifically a risk of harm, or a danger. It was first used for golf hazards in the 1850s.

STYMIE

'Stymie' is a golfing term that has come to have other meanings. A stymie in golf was a situation where your opponent's ball was between your ball and the hole on the putting green, so that you could not make a shot. You could be said to 'stymie' your opponent if you put them in this situation. The word may be related to an old Scots phrase, dating from the 1300s, 'not to see a styme', meaning not to be able to see at all. This in turn may have come from the Vikings, but it is all very unclear. The figurative use of the verb 'stymie' cropped up around the beginning of the 20th century, and has really taken off.

CADDY

Amazingly enough, 'caddy' started out in life as the Latin word *caput*, which means 'head'. A diminutive form of *caput* was *capitetto*, which meant 'little head'. This ended up in the Gascon dialect of French as *capdet*, which meant chief or captain ('captain' also comes from *caput*). These captains from Gascony who served in the French king's army tended to be younger sons of noble families (the older sons inherited and the younger sons joined the army). So when the central French encountered this Gascon word *capdet* in about 1400, they thought it meant 'younger son'. In fact, the French dropped the word they already had for a younger son, *puisné* (literally meaning 'born next'), which survives in English as 'puny', and replaced it with *cadet*. Then in about 1600 the English got hold of the word from the French. The English pronounced it CADDEE in imitation of the French, and for about two hundred years it meant a younger son. But it also gradually came to have military connotations, because in England too, younger sons tended to join the army. Eventually the pronunciation came to reflect the spelling, and this is how we ended up with 'cadet' meaning a student at a military academy.

Meanwhile, however, in Scotland, the pronunciation 'caddee' continued to be used, reflected in the spelling 'caddie'; from 'younger son' the sense shifted to 'young lad', especially one who runs errands or does odd jobs, and from there came to apply to young lads carrying golf clubs. A final interesting development with this word was that a short form of 'caddie'—'cad'—was used by students at Eton to refer to the lower-class lads who acted as ballboys or whatever in their sports. When Etonians moved on to Oxford, they used 'cad' contemptuously to apply to the townsmen of the lower classes generally, and before you knew it, a 'cad' was anyone whose manners or behaviour were disapproved of.

Incidentally, the storage box 'caddy', as in 'tea caddy' or 'shower caddy', is unrelated. It started out as Malay *kati*, which was a unit of weight equal to about six hundred grams. Presumably tea was originally sold in these quantities, and the name shifted from the quantity of tea to the container holding it.

FALL

BACK TO SCHOOL

ॐ

Fall may officially begin on September 22, but psychologically it starts with the return to school. We look at the word 'school' itself, and also school subjects, names for the students, the books and paper they use, the testing they undergo, a few adjectives which can describe the school experience for the hard-working student, and the sneaky ways the lazy ones avoid having to work.

SCHOOL
Unlikely as it may seem to the whining schoolboy creeping unwillingly to school, this word is ultimately from a word meaning 'leisure'! This was the Greek word *skholē*, but since the Greeks were highly cultured people, their idea of leisure was hanging out with Socrates and Plato discussing philosophy, so *skholē* came to mean 'employment of one's leisure time in disputation and discussion'. It later came to apply to more formalized discussion in the ancient Greek equivalent of a school. The Romans borrowed it from the Greeks and almost all European languages borrowed it from Latin. In English, it would have been pronounced SKOLE until Shakespeare's time (the double *o* represents a long *o* in Middle English). There was no *h* in the word in English until the Renaissance, when people wanting to show off their knowledge of Greek and Latin reinserted it.

CURRICULUM
'Curriculum' comes from a Latin word meaning 'race course'. The Latin verb *currere* meant 'to run', and a *curriculum* was a racing chariot or the race course on which they competed. So 'curricular' in English originally meant 'having to do with horse-drawn

carriages'. Which would mean, I guess, that refusing to engage in extra-curricular activities would be refusing to engage in anything other than horse-drawn carriages! However, 'curriculum' came to be applied to education in Scottish universities in the 1600s. I suppose the idea was that the prescribed course of studies was like a race course that students were required to run.

ALGEBRA, ALGORITHM, ARITHMETIC

Like most words starting in *al-*, 'algebra' comes from Arabic. It makes sense that a mathematical term comes from Arabic, because through the Dark Ages a lot of the mathematical learning of the ancient world survived only in Arabic civilization, and Europeans had to learn it from the Arabic mathematicians who were living in Spain at the time. In Arabic, *al-jabr* means 'the reunion of broken parts' or 'bone-setting'. In fact, when the word 'algebra' was first used in English in the 1500s, it meant the surgical treatment of broken bones. So you have to wonder, 'How on earth did it come to mean this thing we study in school?'. The mathematical sense came from the title of a 9th-century Arabic mathematical treatise, *'Ilm al-jabr wa'l mukabala*, which meant 'the science of restoring what is missing and equating like with like'. And when you think about it, solving an algebraic equation is like taking something that's broken into pieces and putting it back together again.

This book, which also introduced Arabic numerals to Europe, was written by a mathematician called Abu Ja'far Mohammed Ben Musa, who was also known as *al-Khowarazmi* (literally 'the native of Khwaraz'). His name has given us the word 'algorithm'. This was 'algorism' when it first entered English in the 1200s, at which time, and for seven centuries afterward, it designated the Arabic numbering system. In the 19th century, 'algorism' passed through what the OED delightfully calls 'pseudo-etymological perversions', one of them being confusion with the Greek word for 'number', *arithmós*, which has given us 'arithmetic'. The current sense of 'algorithm', 'a process, or set of rules, usually one expressed in algebraic notation, now used especially in computing' dates only from the 1930s.

GRAMMAR

The amazing thing is that 'grammar' and 'glamour' started out as one and the same word. 'Grammar' comes ultimately from a Greek word *gramma*, meaning a letter of the alphabet or something written. In theory, 'grammar' in the Middle Ages meant the study of language, but in practice it meant only the study of Latin, because Latin was the only language that was taught using the study of structures. People probably weren't even aware that languages like English, French, and German *had* something that could be called grammar. Many students are probably wishing at this point that we could go back to those innocent days!

Because 'grammar' meant the knowledge or study of Latin, it was also used to mean the knowledge of those who belonged to the learned class, and this knowledge was thought by most people to include magic and astrology. So 'grammar' or 'gramarye' could mean 'magic' or 'occult learning' as well. Yet another variant of this was 'glomery', which the Scots changed to 'glamour' in the early 1700s. So 'glamour' started out in Scots English meaning 'magic' or a spell. Then Sir Walter Scott got hold of it and popularized it, so that soon it meant a magical beauty and finally a kind of highly refined beauty or attractiveness. Now, when I was a teenager, I remember my sister and I used to read a magazine called *Glamour* (you would never tell by looking at me now!), and I bet it wouldn't sell half so well if it were called *Grammar*.

PUPIL

Both 'pupil' the student in school and the pupil of the eye derive from the same Latin word, but took diverging paths to get where they are now. The Latin word was *pupillus*, which meant 'child', but specifically an orphan child, one who was under the care of a guardian. This is what the word meant when it first entered English. In Wycliffe's translation of the Bible in 1384, for instance, people are adjured to 'visit pupils and widows in their tribulacioun'. Two hundred years later, in Shakespeare's time, the word was being used to mean a university student. By the 18th century we find this intriguing description of educational practice: 'She instructs those who are young and spritely among her pupils, to practise the most wild, freakish, wanton and romantic gestures, as to that of indecently stripping themselves, twirling round, extorting their features, shaking and twitching their bodies and limbs into a variety of odd and unusual ways.' Perhaps the whining

schoolboy would creep less snail-like to that particular school!

Meanwhile, the Latin word was also developing along other lines. The feminine form was *pupilla*, which, as well as meaning 'female child', also meant 'doll'. The Romans used this word for the opening in the iris because, if you look into the pupils, tiny reflected images can be seen. The word wasn't borrowed into English in this sense till the 1400s. Before that, the pupil was called the 'black of the eye', or the 'sight' or 'sight-hole', or, way back in Old English, 'the apple of the eye'. The figurative use of 'the apple of someone's eye' dates all the way back to King Alfred the Great's time.

TRUANT

'Truant' comes from a Celtic word meaning 'wretched'. When the word was first used in English, a 'truant' was a beggar. But not just any beggar: it was a term of abuse for an able-bodied person who you thought could be making an honest living instead of pan-handling. Some things never change! Our first evidence of the word, in fact, is a statement that people thought St Francis of Assisi was a 'truant' (1209). That layabout. From the 1300s to the 1600s, it was a general term of abuse for someone perceived as being lazy, and it was applied to children skipping school as early as the 1400s.

GEEK

'Geek' seems to have started out as a variant of 'geck', which was a dialect word for a stupid or peculiar person. Coincidentally, someone is actually referred to as a 'geeke' in Shakespeare's *Cymbeline*, but this is likely just a misspelling of 'geck'. So geek chugged along in the 19th century as a general term of contempt. It acquired a particular meaning in early 20th-century carnival sideshows as a person who performed sensational and disgusting acts like biting heads off chickens. So now there was an element of freakishness added to the meaning of the word. Because students are always on the lookout for slang terms to designate someone who is overly studious and therefore perceived as antisocial, they appropriated 'geek' for this purpose in the 1960s.

NERD

No one really knows about this one for sure. We do know that it can't have come from 'drunk' spelled backwards, or from the name of the ventriloquist's dummy Mortimer Snerd in the 1930s, as some have suggested. It might be a euphemistic alteration of 'turd', but it is also possible that we owe it to Dr Seuss, who in his 1950 book *If I ran the Zoo* penned the immortal line, 'I'll sail to Ka-Troo/And Bring Back... a Nerkle, a Nerd, and a Seersucker too!' The 'nerd' in question is 'depicted as a small, unkempt, humanoid creature with a large head and a comically disapproving expression', to quote the *Oxford English Dictionary*.

DUNCE

The word 'dunce' actually has its origins in the name of a very intelligent and celebrated medieval theologian. This was John Duns Scotus, who lived in the 1200s. He wrote books on theology, philosophy, and logic which were used in all the universities, and he had a huge following. His stature was similar to that of St Thomas Aquinas. But by the 1500s, with the rise of humanism, and in particular the Protestant Reformation, scholastic philosophy as represented by Duns Scotus fell into disrepute, and his followers, known as 'Duns men', were treated with contempt. His detractors said that Duns Scotus's philosophy was riddled with sophistry and ridiculous reasoning. Meanwhile, his followers, who were by now being called 'Dunses' for short, railed against the 'new learning' and clung to the old ways. The adherents of the new philosophy started to use 'Duns' to mean someone who would not—or could not—learn new things.

FOOLSCAP

Speaking of dunces leads us to the classic dunce cap, and from there to another kind of 'cap' used in school. Most people pronounce 'foolscap' like FULLscap. I always thought as a kid that there was an empty scap and a full scap. But the word really is 'fool's cap'. It came to be applied to paper because in the 15th or 16th century a certain papermaker started identifying his paper with a watermark of a jester's cap.

BOOK

'Book' goes back to Anglo-Saxon. It is thought that the word is etymologically related to the beech tree, on which runes were carved, or which provided wooden tablets on which inscriptions could be carved.

TEXT

'Text', like 'textile', comes from the Latin verb *tenere* meaning 'to weave'. *Textus* meant 'woven', or, by metaphorical extension, the structure of a literary work in which many strands are interwoven. The word entered English in the 1300s for the wording of anything written or printed, but its use as a short form for 'textbook' dates only from the 1950s.

ATLAS

Atlases are named after the Greek god who was believed to hold up the pillars of the universe. They are called this because the first book of maps, by Gerard Mercatur in 1636, had an engraving of Atlas holding up the heavens as its frontispiece.

ANTHOLOGY

'Anthology' literally means 'a bunch of flowers'. It comes from the Greek word *anthos* meaning 'flower' (which also turns up in words like 'chrysanthemum') and *logia* meaning 'a collection'. The first anthologies (in Ancient Greek times) were collections of small, choice poems, which were seen as the 'flowers of verse'.

THESAURUS

'Thesaurus' comes from the Greek word for 'treasure house'. When it was first used in English, it applied to any book that was a 'treasure house' of information, such as a dictionary or encyclopedia. In 1852 the English scholar Peter Mark Roget produced a thematically arranged dictionary that he called a 'thesaurus'; as a result, the word has since been restricted to dictionaries of synonyms.

ESSAY

'Essay' comes from the French verb *essayer,* meaning 'to try', which in turn comes from the Latin word *exagium,* which meant 'weighing' but got extended to mean an examination or trial or testing.

So 'essay' did originally mean in English an attempt to do something. Its use for a written composition we owe to the French writer Michel de Montaigne, who published a collection of what he called *Essais* in 1580. This rather self-deprecating title suggested that the pieces lacked finish, that they were just a stab at dealing with the topic (although they're actually extremely well-written). With his *Essais* Montaigne created a new literary genre, and students may curse him for it!

EXAM

The Latin word for the pointer on a pair of scales was *examen*, from which was derived the word *examinare,* meaning 'to weigh accurately in a balance'. But it was obviously a short step for the Romans to go from 'weigh something' to 'consider' or 'inquire into' or 'test the quality of', and all of those senses came into English with the word 'examine' in the 1300s. The notion of 'testing someone's knowledge by questioning' dates from the same time in English. So if, God forbid, one should fail one's exams, it could be said that one has literally been weighed in the balance and found wanting (a phrase that, according to the Biblical book of Daniel, was written by a disembodied hand on the wall of King Nebuchednezzar's banquet hall to put the fear of the Lord into him).

TEST

The Latin word *testa* meant an earthen vessel or pot. This migrated into Old French as *teste*, which was used to mean specifically the metallurgical vessel in which gold or silver was assayed to determine how pure it was. That was the original meaning of the word 'test' in English, but by about Shakespeare's time, it was being used figuratively to mean a trial of the quality or genuineness of anything. So the expression, 'put someone to the test', arose. And you could talk about a test of character and so on. But what's surprising about this word is that its use to mean the act of ascertaining the academic or mental or physiological or personal qualities of a person—a medical test or a French test, for instance—is very recent, no earlier than 1900.

TESTY

Both exams and tests may make students a bit testy, but although 'testy' also comes from the Latin word *testa* meaning 'pot', it came into English by a much more circuitous route than 'test' did. In popular Latin the word *testa* was also a slang word for the head, presumably because the head looks like a pot (whereas the classical Latin word for the head was *caput*). Popular rather than classical Latin determined the evolution of the vocabulary in Romance languages such as French, and that's why the French word for 'head' is *tête*. In Old French this was still pronounced *teste*, and someone who was headstrong was called *testu* (the French word for 'stubborn' is *têtu* still). *Testu* came into Anglo-Norman French (which is what came over to England) as *testif*, which was eventually shortened to 'testy'. 'Testy' originally meant 'headstrong and impetuous', and from there it was just a short step to the current meaning, 'aggressive and short-tempered'.

GRUELLING

Tests and exams are often described as gruelling. How is this related to the unappetizing dish of oatmeal boiled in water—a kind of porridge soup—known as 'gruel'? We got the word 'gruel' from French in the 1300s when it meant any ground grain (if you look on your bag of Quaker Oats you will see that to this day in Canadian French *gruau* is the word for ground oats). Just as *gruau* in French can also mean the porridge made from the oats, so 'gruel' in English came to mean this broth including boiled oats. Now, gruel was not exactly a gourmet delicacy. So a phrase arose in the 1700s, 'get one's gruel', which meant to be punished or even to be killed. And from this arose a short-lived verb 'to gruel' meaning to exhaust or to disable, which now survives only in the adjective 'gruelling'.

METICULOUS
A good student will be meticulous, possibly from fear of failing, and 'meticulous' does come from a word meaning 'fear': the Latin *metus*. When it came into English in the 1500s, 'meticulous' meant fearful and timid. Oddly, there seems to have been a gap in the language between about 1700 and 1800, and then in the early 1800s we find the word being used again but in a slightly different sense, more like 'fearful of making a mistake, overly careful about minute details'. It definitely had negative connotations though, more like 'nitpicky' than what we now understand as meticulous, which seems to date only from the 1950s.

PLAGIARISM
'Plagiarism' comes from a Latin word *plagiarius*, which meant 'kidnapper'. It was used by the Romans to mean someone who stole or abducted someone else's child or slave, especially (so the implication is) for prostitution or some other debauched purpose. I have no idea whether this was a really common problem in ancient Rome, but they had a word for it, so it must have been a problem of some significance. Even back then, the Romans also used this word to mean the stealing or copying of a literary work, so I guess they thought of a literary work as being someone's child. I talk about my dictionary as being my 'baby', so I guess that makes sense. When the word was borrowed from Latin into English about 1600, it wasn't 'plagiarism', but 'plagiary', and it did mean a kidnapper. But after about a hundred years that sense died out, leaving us with only the sense of intellectual theft. And of course 'plagiarism' won out over 'plagiary'.

CHEAT
'Cheat' has travelled a very long way from its origins in Latin prop-

erty law. It can be traced ultimately to the Latin word *excadere*, which meant essentially 'to become a person's property'. In Old French this verb *excadere* got squished down to *eschete,* which meant an inheritance, in other words, what became a person's property on someone's death. When this crossed the Channel into English, it came to have a slightly different meaning. In feudal law, the French word was *eschete*, and in English it was 'escheat'; an escheat was when someone's property reverted to their feudal lord or the Crown on their death instead of going to their heirs. Sometimes this happened because there were no heirs, but often the property was confiscated as punishment for a crime. So the beneficiaries of the will were done out of their property when they were escheated. Now, 'escheat' isn't very easy to say, and soon it was shortened to 'cheat'. By Shakespeare's time it had taken on a broader sense of depriving anyone of anything, especially unjustly or by deceit. In another hundred years after that, the idea of acting deceitfully had become so strong that the word 'cheat' came to have its modern meaning of acting dishonestly to achieve an unfair advantage. In the 20th-century development of this word, it can mean acting deceitfully in any circumstance, as in cheating on one's spouse. We now even talk about 'cheating' on a diet, which just reflects the whole moral attitude to weight which developed in 20th-century society.

GAMES CHILDREN PLAY

ɞ

With the kids back in school, schoolyards at recess resound with the clamour of kids playing traditional games that even the advent of video games has failed to eradicate.

HOPSCOTCH

You might think that there's some cute story about Scotch whisky involved with 'hopscotch'. In fact, it has nothing whatsoever to do with the Scots. 'Scotch' meaning Scottish goes back only to the 1600s, whereas the 'scotch' that turns up in 'hopscotch' goes back to the 1400s. This was a verb that meant 'to cut a line in' or 'to make a gash in'. We don't know where it came from into English but one thing's for sure, it has nothing to do with Scotland. We have a cookbook from 1450 recommending that fish to be grilled should be 'skoched' first (today we would say 'scored'). If you think of what a piece of steak that has been scored with a knife looks like, you can see the resemblance to a hopscotch drawing on a sidewalk. 'Hopscotch' means 'hop over the lines', more or less. In fact, the earliest references to it, in 1688, called it 'hop skotches'.

Meanwhile, however, 'scotch' went on to acquire other meanings. In *Macbeth* we find a line 'We have scotch'd the snake, not killed it', meaning 'we have inflicted some harm on it as if we'd gashed it with a knife'. This became a popular catchphrase 'to scotch but not kill', so that by the 1800s, 'scotch' meant 'stamp out something dangerous, especially an idea', and by the beginning of the 20th century, 'scotch' was being used to mean 'refute or nullify', as in 'scotch a rumour' or 'scotch an attempt'. So nothing to do with Scots, which just goes to show you that you shouldn't leap to conclusions about words that look or sound the same as other words.

RED ROVER

Red Rover seems to be a game that we acquired from the Scots (like so many things in Canada and Canadian English). It may have originally been called 'Jockie Rover', but 'Red Rover' was the name of a notorious pirate in a novel of the same name by James Fenimore Cooper in 1827. The same character also turns up in *The Fair Maid of Perth*. It's not surprising that children would find the name of a pirate more exciting than 'Jockie Rover'.

The word 'rove' started out meaning 'shoot arrows randomly', without necessarily aiming at a target. This was supposed to give archers practice at judging the distance of the target. Not surprisingly, people living in cities in the Middle Ages didn't appreciate having archers shooting off arrows without aiming at something in particular, so the first evidence of the word 'rove' is from a bylaw in Coventry banning the practice. People were complaining that their hedges were getting bashed up! By the 1500s, 'rove' had acquired its present meaning of wandering about without any particular destination in mind, much like the arrows.

DOLL, DOLLY

'Dolly' was originally a nickname for a person called Dorothy, much as 'Sally' is derived from Sarah and 'Molly' from Mary. This, shortened to 'doll' is the origin of the name of the child's toy resembling a human figure, which started to be called that in the late 1600s. Before this, in the 1500s, the words 'puppet', 'poppet', and 'moppet' had been used, but it is unclear what dolls were called before that.

MARBLE, ALLY

'Marble' comes ultimately from a Greek word *marmaros,* meaning 'shining stone'. In fact, the Sea of Marmara, which connects the Black Sea to the Aegean, is called this because marble has been quarried there since ancient times. Although kids have probably been playing marbles since at least the Middle Ages, we don't find the game called 'marbles' until the 1600s. Originally the little balls were indeed made of marble.

'Ally', in the marble sense, which we first find mentioned by Daniel Defoe in 1720, is a short form of 'alabaster', designating the fancy marbles made of alabaster or real marble instead of the cheap ones made of terracotta. 'Alabaster' comes quite simply from the Greek word for this kind of gypsum, *alabastros.*

TEEN-SPEAK

ॐ

Every new school year brings new teen slang with it. The whole point of teen slang is to exclude those who don't speak it, so by necessity it has to change from year to year. Some usages that we think started out recently in teen slang go surprisingly far back, and have migrated into the vocabulary of most English speakers.

LIKE
'Like, wow' or 'He's like the most fabulous hunk I've ever seen'. These are both instances of 'like' used as an intensifier, which it is in ordinary speech. People tend to think of words like this as having appeared somewhat suddenly about ten years ago. But interestingly, the earliest evidence we have for 'like' being used as an intensifier is from 1778 in the English novelist Fanny Burney's *Evelina*. Now, in British English, 'like' comes *after* the word being intensified. So Fanny Burney said, 'Father grew quite uneasy, like, for fear of his lordship's taking offence.' We would say, 'He got, like, really upset'. But the 'like' is performing exactly the same semantic function. Fanny Burney was being a valley girl but backwards, so to speak. Who knew. Another use of 'like' is the phrase 'be like', meaning 'to say': 'And I was, like, "Oh my God"' or 'She's like, "Isn't he incredible?"'. The earliest evidence we have of this is from Frank Zappa's 'Valley Girl', so it does seem to be from valley-girl slang, but it obviously is used more widely now.

GO
People who think that saying, 'And I'm going, "I can't believe it"' is highly illiterate will no doubt be surprised to learn that our

first evidence for 'go' meaning 'to say' comes from, wait for it, Charles Dickens. Obviously 'go' has been in the language for ages with many senses. One of those, starting in about 1700, was 'to make a sound'. Now, originally, this was used of animals or non-human things: 'The cow went "moo"', 'The sheep went "baa"', 'The clock went "tic-toc"'. Then in the 1800s we find this quote from Dickens, in *The Pickwick Papers*: '"Yo, yo, yo, yo, yoe," went the first boy.' Dickens was not the first person to use it of a human; it's just the first place that we've been able to find it. But for about the first hundred years, 'go' meaning 'say' was always with odd or inarticulate sounds like, 'yo, yo', or 'chip, chip' or 'hmm, hmm'. It's only much more recently that we have it meaning 'say' in more common contexts. The earliest quotation we have for that is from 1942, and it does seem to have arisen in teen slang: 'So he goes, "Well, what did you do?" and I go, "I didn't do nothing."' Highly literate. But it's a very handy word, 'go', so this usage has caught on.

AS IF

Our first quotation for this is another surprisingly early one, in a novel published in 1903 called *The Pit*: '"Maybe he'll come up and speak to us." "Oh, as if," contradicted Laura.' Then we have a huge gap, because our next quotation is from 1981, in a listing of University of North Carolina slang. By the 1990s it was being used in movies like *Wayne's World* and *Clueless*. So there's early evidence of this phrase but it has become widespread only recently.

DUH

When we were editing the letter 'D' for the first edition of the *Canadian Oxford Dictionary* in 1993, we wrote an entry for the word 'duh', which at the time was used to suggest that the person uttering it was mentally slow. The earliest example we have is from a *Merry Melodies* cartoon in 1943: 'Duh… Well, he can't outsmart me, 'cause I'm a moron.' But the way it's used currently is to imply that *another* person (often the person being talked *to*) is mentally slow or has said something foolish or extremely obvious. This is fairly recent in widespread use. It may surprise people to know that the *Oxford English Dictionary* is interested in *Merry Melodies* cartoons! It sounds like too much fun, as if we sit around watching Roadrunner and Daffy Duck all day. But cartoon scripts are among the many sources that OED lexicographers look at in their search for the earliest source for a word.

SHALL WE DANCE?

ॐ

Buttocks. Bonfires. Beech trees. Goats. Unlikely sources, you might think, for words having to do with the graceful world of ballet. As the new school year gears up, little girls (and not so little ones, like me) and a regrettably small number of boys embark on a new year of ballet classes, while the professional ballet companies start their seasons.

CALLIPYGIAN

Now there's a fine word for you. Barely had the *Canadian Oxford Dictionary* arrived from the printers before a fellow ballet student of mine asked if 'callipygian' was in it. No, I said, it was too rare for a dictionary of this size, but we did have the related 'steatopygia'. Later I was recounting this when giving a talk about the dictionary to a grade nine class. 'Oh,' said their teacher, 'now that might come in handy when we go to the ballet next month.' So what does this word mean? Is it some nifty new dance move?

Some technical ballet term known only to initiates? No, in fact, 'callipygian' means 'having beautiful buttocks'! Well, you can see how it might come in handy! Most of us audience dwellers, however, are unfortunately afflicted by its opposite, 'steatopygia', which is the condition of having excess fat on the buttocks. 'Callipygian' comes to us from the Greek *kallos,* meaning 'beautiful' (which also crops up in 'calligraphy') and *puge,* meaning 'buttocks'.

TUTU
The first real ballet term I want to discuss does, coincidentally, mean 'buttocks'. 'Tutu' was euphemistic baby talk in 19th century French for *cucu,* a derivative of *cul,* a rather coarse word for the backside. It was originally applied to the tight-fitting underwear worn by dancers and then to the dress covering the underwear.

ADAGE
Any dancer will probably snort in derision when told that the word 'adage' (pronounced adAZH) means 'at ease'. Of course, those slow flowing exercises are supposed to look easy, but as anyone knows who's tried one, the dancer is probably thinking, as one of my ballet teachers put it, 'God, I *hate* adage! It's so *hard*!! My hips hurt!' But indeed the word comes to us via French from the Italian *ad agio,* meaning 'at ease' or 'at leisure'. One of the most notoriously difficult challenges in the ballerina's repertoire is the Rose Adagio from *The Sleeping Beauty*. No leisure there!

ENTRECHAT
An entrechat seems, to anyone who knows French, to mean 'between the cats'. This is intriguing, because I've never seen my cats jump straight upwards and beat their little paws in the air (but then I've never seen them point their toes at their knees in a pas de chat either). In fact, 'entrechat' is a French corruption of

the Italian phrase *capriola intrecciata*, meaning literally a 'complicated caper'. *Intrecciata* comes from the word *treccia*, meaning a tress or braid, and this is a clearer image of what the legs do in an entrechat.

CABRIOLE

Another type of jump in which the legs are beaten in a type of scissor kick is the cabriole, which seems to have nothing to do with animals, but in fact derives from the Latin word for 'goat', *capra*. It migrated into Italian as *capriola*, a young goat or fawn, and from there into French as *capriole* or *cabriole*. I don't imagine any of Canada's fine dancers would appreciate being described as 'goat-like', no matter how well they executed their cabrioles.

PIROUETTE, FOUETTÉ

Moving on to turns, a pirouette was originally, in medieval France, a child's spinning top or hand-held windmill. The French word was derived from the Italian *piro*, meaning a peg or pin, and was possibly influenced by another French word, *rouet*, meaning a spinning wheel.

Fouettés are a spectacular type of pirouette, best known in the Black Swan pas de deux, in which the ballerina whips her raised leg around in a kind of eggbeater motion while also spinning on her other leg. The word 'fouetté' can be traced ultimately back to the Latin name for the beech tree, *fagus*, which in Old French became *fou* (not to be confused with the modern French word *fou* meaning crazy, though one might think that a more appropriate description of the movement). A *fouet* was a young or small beech tree and then a stick of beech wood used for beating, before finally settling down to its modern meaning 'whip', which describes the action of the working leg in a fouetté.

BOURRÉE

There is an all-purpose filler connecting dance step called the 'pas de bourrée'. Its etymology is very appropriate, for it comes ultimately from the Latin *burra*, which was coarse wool used for stuffing. In French this became *bourre*, a bundle of twigs with such stuffing, used for bonfires. But what is the connection with dance?

In 1565 a country dance from Auvergne became the rage at the French court; it was a dance traditionally performed around a bonfire and thus called a *bourrée*.

ON STAGE

❧

The fall also sees the beginning of the theatrical season. Here we look at some words related to the theatre, as well as some that started in the theatre but have moved beyond it.

THEATRE
It is not surprising that ancient Greek has contributed many theatrical words to English, including the word 'theatre' itself. It comes ultimately from the verb *theasthai,* meaning 'behold'; a theatre was literally a 'place for viewing'.

PERSON
Theatre seems to be so necessary a part of the human condition that even our word 'person' has its roots in theatre. In Latin a *persona* was originally the mask worn by actors, before it came to mean a character in a play and then any human individual. This came into English via French in about the 1200s. Of course, the Anglo-Saxons did have a word to designate human beings of either sex, but this was the rather ill-fated 'man', which is beating an ever-hastier retreat in all but its strictly masculine senses as the Latinate (and theatrical) 'person' takes over. At least 'person' has pleasant connotations, which is more than can be said for the word English has borrowed from the Greek word for actor—'hypocrite'!

TRAGEDY

'Tragedy', meanwhile, has one of the world's most intriguing un-solved etymologies. We know that the Greek word for tragedy was *tragoidia*. This comes from two words, *oide* meaning 'song' or 'ode' and *tragos* meaning… 'goat'.

Yes, goat. (Attentive readers will begin to think that goats are a recurring theme, since they turned up in our discussion of 'cabri-ole' and other ballet words, and also in our discussion of taxis.) No one knows why on earth a tragedy was called a 'goat song'. One suggestion is that perhaps a goat was given as a prize at an ancient Greek drama festival, but this has not been confirmed.

COMEDY

'Comedy', on the other hand, is less mystifying. It has the same element, *oide* meaning 'song', but its first element, *comos*, simply meant merry-making.

FARCE

A particular type of comedy is the farce. In the early Middle Ages, much of the theatre was based on religious subjects and could therefore be quite serious and morally uplifting in tone. Not surprisingly, the actors, and even more likely the audience, felt the need for some light relief, so gradually comic interludes, very often made up of slapstick and buffoonery, were inserted into the serious plays to lighten things up. The French, who even then were obsessed with food, equated these interludes with the stuffing in a roast chicken, so used their word for 'stuffing', *farce*, for them. Eventually, of course, people enjoyed the comic bits so much that farces came to stand on their own as comic plays.

SOCK

Even socks started out in the theatre! 'Socks' were originally not what we know as socks, but rather light, low-heeled shoes or slippers. The Latin word *soccus* meant particularly a light shoe worn by comic actors. Tragic actors wore heavy boots called buskins (which did *not* give us the word 'busker', but that's another story), whereas comic actors wore these light shoes. This is one of those rare words borrowed into Old English from Latin, long before the French invaded England. We have evidence of it from 725 to mean 'a shoe'. It wasn't until the 1300s, however, that 'sock' was used for the item of hosiery. Until then the word 'hose' had been used.

PANTS

Pants as in 'trousers', not as in 'heavy breathing' (for which see BATTER UP!, page 126). 'Pants' is a shortening of the word 'pantaloon'. Pantaloon was the name of a Venetian character in *commedia dell'arte*, which was a theatrical form in about the 1600s or 1700s. Pantaloon was an old man—one of those stock characters—who wore close-fitting, full-length breeches. The stage character's name was in turn derived from the name of an obscure saint, St Pantaleon, who was much venerated in Venice. The name was associated with this person who had this specific costume, and trousers were called 'pantaloons' by about 1800. The shortened form, 'pants', was already in use by 1840.

PLAUDIT

When speaking of the theatre, it is only appropriate to finish off with a round of applause, and this convention, which dates back to Roman times at least, has given the language a word that is now used only outside theatrical circles. It was the tradition in the Roman theatre for the actors to say, '*Plaudite!*' to the audience at the end of a play. This was in effect an order to applaud! This word is the root of our word 'plaudit', which originally was a literal round of applause at a play. The figurative—and now only—use of 'plaudit' dates only from the 19th century.

MUSIC TO OUR EARS

ॐ

Like the ballet and theatre companies, orchestras start their seasons up again in the fall.

ORCHESTRA

There is no truth to the rumour that 'orchestra' is derived from the Greek word for 'testicle'. 'Orchid' is, but that's a different story!

'Orchestra' comes from the Greek word *orkheisthai,* meaning 'to dance'. The orchestra was originally the space in front of an ancient Greek theatre stage where the chorus danced and sang. No one really knows where *orkheisthai* comes from, but there's a theory that it may be related to a Sanskrit word meaning 'tremble'. The word 'orchestra' came into English in the late 1500s, reflecting the Renaissance interest in things classical. For the first hundred or so years of its existence in English it referred only to the ancient Greek or Roman theatre. What we think of as an orchestra, with combined groups of different kinds of instruments, arose in Italy during the course of the 1600s, as a musical group to accompany operas and ballets. The most logical place to put the musicians for these performances was in front of the stage, and indeed orchestra pits were a standard feature of Italian opera-house architecture by the 1680s. Since this location was analogous to the 'orchestra' in a Greek theatre, we started to use the word 'orchestra' for it, and then by extension for the musicians who played there.

SYMPHONY

'Symphony' comes from the Greek elements *syn-* meaning 'together' and *phone* meaning 'sound'. It popped up in English fairly early, in the 1200s. We borrowed it from the French, and it was used very vaguely throughout the Middle Ages to designate various musical instruments, and possibly as a synonym for 'musical instrument' itself, since 'instrument' meant something else back then. From about 1400 on, 'symphony' meant 'harmony' or 'harmonious music'. By the mid-1600s it was being applied to a specific type of instrumental musical composition which evolved through the classical period into the symphony as we know it. The term 'symphony orchestra' was, it would seem, created for the founding of the Boston Symphony Orchestra in 1881. This probably reflects the increasing importance of the symphony as a musical genre during the 19th century, and was a way of indicating the presumably large size of the orchestra—that is, that it wasn't a chamber orchestra.

PHILHARMONIC

'Philharmonic' comes from two Greek words meaning 'love' and 'harmony'. Its use to describe a musical organization dates from the mid-1700s, when there was a Philharmonic Society in Dublin. The Philharmonic Society of London (now the Royal Philharmonic Society) was founded in 1813. This was the organization that commissioned Beethoven's Ninth Symphony, and in their founding documents they stated that their goal was 'to procure the performance, in the most perfect manner possible, of the best and most approved Instrumental Music'. This Society garnered a lot of prestige, and throughout the 1800s many new orchestras sprang up with 'philharmonic' in their title, among them the New York and Vienna Philharmonics in 1842 and the Berlin Philharmonic in 1882. The success of 'philharmonic' is in part also due to the fact that it can be applied to both choral and instrumental ensembles.

INSTRUMENT

'Instrument' derives ultimately from a Latin word *struere,* meaning 'pile up'. A derivative of this, *instruere*, which is also the root of our word 'instruct', came to mean 'build' or 'equip' (its opposite, *destruere*, gave us 'destroy'), and an *instrumentum* was a tool for building or any item of equipment. So in early English, the word 'instrument' can be found referring to ladders and scaffolding. But eventually it was restricted to musical instruments or other finely tuned or delicate devices. And here is a quotation from an account book of 1540, to show that, for musicians, some things never change: 'Paid to ye clarke for playeng of ye yensterment: 4 pence.'

FIDDLE, VIOLIN, VIOL

The mainstay of an orchestra is the string section, and the violin has pride of place. 'Violin' and 'fiddle' both come from the same Latin word, *vitulari*, meaning 'be joyful' or 'celebrate a festival'. This in turn may come from the name of a Roman goddess, Vitula, who was the goddess of joy and victory. What a wonderful idea, to have a goddess of joy! All the Romance and Germanic languages borrowed *vitula* to designate some kind of stringed musical instrument. The Anglo-Saxons brought the word across to England as *fithele*. This carried on quite happily for several centuries with no informal connotations, but meanwhile, the Norman French invaded England. The French too had had their way with *vitula*; typically dropping the consonant out of the middle to end up with *vielle*, which in turn became 'viol'. Because French words were more prestigious than Anglo-Saxon ones in medieval England, the honourable pedigree of 'fiddle' was soon under attack. And then 'violin' came into the language from Italian in the late 1500s. In music, things Italian were very prestigious, so we stuck with 'violin', though it has never been able to oust 'fiddle' entirely. Indeed, classical violinists are known to refer affectionately to their instruments as fiddles. The phrase 'play second fiddle' dates from the 1780s, and 'as fit as a fiddle' from the 1600s. A delightful obsolete expression is 'have a face made of a fiddle', meaning to be irresistibly charming.

THE HUNT IS ON

&

Humans have always been hunters, so hunting words have been with us for a long time. And there are also words in the language that started out in hunting but have since lost their connection with it.

QUARRY

'Quarry' is a word we got in the Middle Ages from the French word *cuirée,* which in turn came from the Latin word *corium* for 'skin'. What happened was, when people went hunting in the Middle Ages, after they had killed their deer, they would place the deer's heart and liver on a piece of its hide and let the dogs eat it as a reward. (There's a cheery thought if you're snacking while reading this!) It was only in the 1600s that the word came to mean the animal being hunted or, figuratively, anything sought after.

This has nothing to do with the stone quarry, which comes ultimately from the Latin *quadrum* meaning 'square', since stone is cut into square pieces.

VENISON

'Venison' also comes from Latin. *Venation* meant 'hunting' in Latin, and that came from *venari,* 'to hunt'. We borrowed it from the French in the Middle Ages and, interestingly, at that time, it didn't mean 'deer' in particular, it meant any kind of food caught by hunting. So it could be deer, or rabbit, or wild boar, or even bear meat or swan. This remained the case until late into the 1600s. We even have a quotation for 'kangaroo venison' from as recently as 1852! Originally it was the lower classes who applied 'venison' specifically to deer (they probably weren't hunting swans) and eventually this 'deer' sense came to take over from the others.

RED HERRING

A red herring was originally a smoked herring, because the smoking caused the fish to turn a reddish colour. Red herrings were used to train hunting dogs to follow a scent. As you can imagine, a smoked herring is quite smelly. Of course, the dogs wouldn't have been hunting for fish, but sometimes dead foxes weren't available for training purposes. So red herrings were used instead. Now, as you can imagine, if you have a pack of hounds chasing a fox and a red herring is drawn across the trail, it's going to distract the hounds from their original object. So that's why 'red herring' came to mean 'something distracting' in the late 1800s.

SLEUTH

'Sleuth' is a very old word. It comes to us from Old Norse, which is what the Vikings spoke when they arrived in England. In Old Norse, the word *slóth* meant a track or trail. When this was borrowed into English in the 1200s, it meant specifically the trail of a hunted animal. By the 1400s, the compound 'sleuth dog' or 'sleuth hound' had arisen, meaning a dog used for tracking, especially a bloodhound. Like many Old Norse words, this one was found mostly in Scottish English from the 1200s to the 1400s, because Scotland was where the Norse people settled. But then it died out for 500 years until revived, like so many archaisms, by Sir Walter Scott. The detective sense, which was a creative extension from the bloodhound, arose in the late 1800s.

POTSHOT

'Potshot' originally designated a shot taken by a hunter whose sole intention was to bag something for dinner, something for the 'pot'. Nowadays, I think it's considered ethical to hunt for food. But back in the mid-1880s, if you just took a shot at anything you saw, hoping that it would be your dinner, you would be regarded with opprobrium by hunters who felt that certain rules of the sport or skill should come into play. It just wasn't the done thing. Often 'potshot' was used to describe a situation where the hunter would shoot without aiming into a crowd of partridges or whatever. The 'criticism' sense dates from the early 20th century.

THANKSGIVING

The second Monday in October, and it's time to tuck into some hearty fare, and the words that describe it.

TURKEY

Why is a turkey called a turkey if it doesn't come from Turkey? 'Turkey' is a shortened form of 'turkey cock' or 'turkey hen'. The first bird to be called a turkey cock was what we now call a guineafowl (as if we weren't geographically confused enough already). This was an African bird ('Guinea' back then applied to the west coast of Africa in general), which was imported through Turkey or at least through the Ottoman Empire, which extended through North Africa (and was thought of as Turkey since it was under Turkish control). 'Turkey' was a kind of grab bag for everything exotic, so when the English settlers arrived in America and saw this native American fowl which, like the guineafowl, had wattles and a featherless neck and head, they called it a turkeycock as well (much as they used the word 'robin' to designate a North American thrush that has nothing in common with an English robin except for its red breast).

BIRD

'Bird' in Old English meant only the young of feathered creatures, sort of like 'kitten' for cats. The generic word for feathered things was 'fowl'. 'Bird' in this sense started out in the north of England, then crept gradually southward till, by about Chaucer's time, it was being used to mean not only young fowl, but also small adult fowl, until finally it supplanted 'fowl' almost entirely. For a while before this happened, 'bird' was also used for the young of other animals and even of humans. In fact, it was a quite respectful synonym for a young girl. So we have a 1300s quotation referring to the Virgin Mary as a 'bird', which is quite incongruous to our ears!

HERB

Turkey or bird, it wouldn't taste so good without a stuffing rich in herbs. Canadians are about evenly split on how to pronounce this word, with a slight edge for the *h*-ful pronunciations. Some people believe that saying ERB (as Americans do) for 'herb' is 'bad pronunciation'. But it is those who say ERB who have history on their side.

The word came into English from the French *erbe* after the Norman Conquest. The French had got the word from the Latin *herba*, but in Late Latin, *h*'s were silent, so this was pronounced *erba* (AIRba). The Old French didn't bother putting in silent letters, so *erbe* it was. And in fact, the word was spelled 'erbe' in English from about 1200 to about 1475, and of course there was no *h* sound because there was no *h* letter! But by the late 1400s there was an upsurge of interest in classical languages, and people started spelling the word with an *h* again to reflect its Latin origins. However, the *h* in 'herb' was still not pronounced, and remained mute until the 19th century in England, at which time it started being pronounced under the influence of the spelling. A number of other *h*-words like 'history' and 'hotel' also started out with silent *h*'s which later came to be pronounced; this is why some people still think (incorrectly) that it is necessary to say 'an historical account' rather than 'a historical account'.

The chronology explains why Americans use the *h*-less pronunciation, because America was settled by English-speakers starting in the 1600s, when 'herb' would have been still pronounced with a mute *h* everywhere in the English-speaking world. And pronunciation features tend to get frozen in time when a people moves to another continent. Canadian English has its roots in the English spoken by Loyalists when they moved north after the American Revolution, bringing with them 'American' pronunciations, so many of us still say ERB. But in the late 19th century, there was a great campaign to make Canadian English more British, as well as a large influx of British immigrants, and this probably accounts for those of us who say HERB. Personally, as an *h*-ful herb person, I am always a little taken aback when I hear ERB. But as a lexicographer, I just recognize that such multiple pronunciations are one of the delightful things about Canadian English, and so typical of the way Canadian English accepts two linguistic standards. Both pronunciations are included in the *Canadian Oxford Dictionary*. Neither is 'bad'.

THYME

The ancient Greek word for thyme was *thumon*, which derived from their verb meaning to burn as a sacrifice. This was because they burned thyme for incense in their temples. This is another of those words where the spelling is quite unnecessarily influenced by the etymology: the *h* is in there only because some busybodies felt that they had to show off that they knew how it was spelled in Greek. Shakespeare actually spelled it 'time' in *A Midsummer Night's Dream*.

PUMPKIN

'Pumpkin', surprisingly, started out in ancient Greek as *pepon*, which meant a large melon. By the time it had migrated through Latin and French, it ended up in English in Tudor times as *pompon* or *pompion*. For some reason, this got changed to 'pumpkin' when the English settlers adapted it to designate the new squash (related to melons) which they found in America. The change is a bit mysterious, because the suffix '-kin' usually implied something small. Maybe it was used by analogy with bumpkin. Who knows? In any case, almost the first use of this word, from 1654, is in reference to pumpkin pie. The only earlier evidence is a rather intriguing mention of someone's 'pumpkin-blasted brains' which one can only conclude is what happens if you eat too much pie at Thanksgiving.

SPICE

'Spice', without which a pumpkin pie would be pretty darned bland, comes from the Latin word *species* (which has also given us, not surprisingly, 'species' and 'specie'), which meant 'a kind, a type'. In the plural, this word in Latin meant 'wares' or 'merchandise'. Since spices were a very important trade commodity, they constituted a major part of a merchant's wares, and gradually the word *species* (which became *espice* in Old French) was restricted from any kind of merchandise to the aromatic vegetable substances we know as spices.

CREAM

Where would pumpkin pie be without a generous dollop of whipped cream? 'Cream' is a word you would expect to go back to Old English, like almost all other dairy-product words, such as 'milk', 'cheese', 'skim', 'curd', 'butter', and so on. But in fact, 'cream' didn't crop up in English till the 1300s. So, first of all, you have to wonder what the Anglo-Saxons called the stuff, since they obviously knew it existed. Their word was *fliete*, which was related to 'float', because cream floats on top of milk. And then 'cream' came along from French. We probably ended up using the French word because cream is, after all, a luxury product, and the French were the ruling class in medieval England.

Where the French got it is an interesting story. They crossed a Gaulish word which meant 'cream' with the Latin word *chrisma*, which meant 'an oil for anointing'. In particular, *chrisma* was a specially consecrated oil mixed with balm and used in certain sacraments such as baptism and confirmation. 'Chrism' has this meaning still today in English. Since cream is a fatty substance, the French took this Latin word meaning 'oil' and applied it to 'oil of milk', so to speak. In *Piers Ploughman* in 1362 we have a very appetizing reference to cottage cheese as 'cruds and cream'. Somehow I don't think we'll be seeing that in any advertisements for cottage cheese!

BATTER UP!

&

Canadian Thanksgiving usually coincides roughly with the World Series. Time to look at some sporting words.

FAN

Fans of baseball and other sports can have a fervour that verges on the religious, which is not surprising in view of the origins of the word. It was, in fact, in reference to baseball that the word 'fan', as a shortened form of 'fanatic', was first used in the 1880s, before being extended to other sports and then to the theatre and other activities. 'Fanatic' is derived from the Latin word *fanaticus* meaning literally 'pertaining to a temple' (the Latin word for 'temple' being *fanum*). But *fanaticus* also had an extended meaning: 'inspired by orgiastic rites, frantic with religious enthusiasm'. I don't know if the World Series can be described as an 'orgiastic rite', but fans can certainly get frantic.

SPORT
Although anyone looking at the Olympics or professional sport these days realizes that sport is a very serious business indeed, the original meaning of 'sport' was 'any pleasing or amusing pastime', not necessarily involving athletic activity. In the 1400s, when the word first appeared, it was the equivalent of what we would call 'fun'. It was a shortened form of the word 'disport', which came into Middle English from Old French, meaning 'a pastime, amusement, recreation'. This came from Latin *dis* meaning 'away' and *portare* meaning 'to carry', the idea being that amusement carried one away from serious or sad occupations, in much the same way that a 'diversion' is literally something that 'turns you away' from other matters.

ROSTER
In Dutch, from which we borrowed this word, *rooster* (pronounced ROASTER) was originally a roasting pan. Specifically it was applied to a gridiron for roasting meat on. The Dutch then extended the meaning of the word to mean a list drawn up in tabular form, because of the similarity of the parallel lines on the paper to a gridiron. Adopted into English in the early 1700s, 'roster' meant a list showing the rotation of duties of soldiers. By the mid-1800s it meant any list of persons or a group of persons who could be considered as a list, for instance the members of an opera company or sports team.

ATHLETE
'Athlete' comes ultimately from the Greek *athlos*, a competition for a prize. It entered English in the Renaissance. Our first quotation

is from a 1528 how-to health book and sounds like an advertisement from the Pork Marketing Board: 'Porke nourisheth most, whereof those that be called athlete have best experience.' I guess even then athletes were used for celebrity endorsement!

CHAMPION

'Champion' comes ultimately from the Latin word *campus* meaning 'field'. A *campio* in Latin was a fighter in a field of athletic or military exercise. From Latin the word migrated to French and from there into English. In fact, two French forms came into English, the central French *champion* and the northern French *campion*, but *campion* has survived only as a family name. Originally a champion was any brave fighter. It wasn't till the 1700s that it meant specifically the winner in sports, and was first used of cricket.

DOPING

'Dope' comes from Dutch *doop* meaning a sauce, or the action of dipping, from the Dutch verb *doopen* meaning 'to dip'. It arose in mid-19th-century American English meaning any thick fluid or semi-liquid substance. Opium as it is prepared for smoking is a thick treacly substance, so the word 'dope' came to apply to it, and by extension to any narcotic substance or drug. This also accounts for the 'stupid person' sense of 'dope', since drug addicts, or anyone who acted as if they were on drugs, were also called 'dopes'. Performance-enhancing substances (as administered to racehorses, not to athletes) were first referred to as 'dope' in 1900, but surprisingly enough, there is a mention of doped athletes as early as 1913. Here it is: 'Doped athletes... It is well-known that the Russian skaters take such stimulants.' The 'stimulant' in question was strychnine!

STAMINA

You could say that the success of an athlete who relies on his or her own stamina rather than on performance-enhancing drugs is literally in the hands of the Fates. *Stamina* is the plural of the Latin word *stamen*, meaning 'thread', which of course has given us the word for the threadlike part of a flower. But *stamen* was also used to mean the thread spun by the three Fates in Greek and Roman mythology, the length of which determined one's life. When 'stamina' first came into English around 1700, it was as the plural of this word 'stamen'. Maintaining the metaphor of the thread spun by the Fates, it meant all the bodily characteristics that could be expected to determine one's life expectancy. That sense died out, leaving us with the current meaning, the capacity to endure fatigue and exertion. The word ceased to be plural and became a singular. Knowing this may come in handy the next time someone berates you for using 'media' or 'data' with a singular verb. Would they say 'Elvis Stojko's stamina *are* extraordinary'?

PANT

An athlete who lacks stamina will be short of breath and panting. Amazingly enough (or perhaps not so amazingly) the word 'pant', meaning 'be breathless', is related etymologically to the word 'fantasy'. They both derive ultimately from the Greek word *phantasia,* which meant 'something made visible'. The Romans borrowed the Greek word to mean 'a nightmare', and created a verb *phantasiare* (in popular Latin *pantasiare*) to mean 'suffer from a nightmare'. When you are awoken from a really bad nightmare, you tend to be gasping for breath, as a result of fear, and thus by the time the Latin word had migrated to French as *pantiser*, it meant 'be short of breath, have difficulty breathing'. The English borrowed *pantiser* in the 1400s, mistaking the –*iser* ending for the suffix '-ize', so shortened it to 'pant'. (For the other 'pant', see On Stage, page 112.)

COACH

To find the origins of the word 'coach', we have to go to Hungary. It is one of very few words in English of Hungarian origin. In the late 1400s, in a Hungarian town called Kocs (pronounced COTCH), the carriage makers came up with a new design for a carriage, which they called a *kocsi szeker* or 'Kocz cart'. We don't know exactly what the new development was, but it must have been the Mercedes-Benz of its day, because it spread like wildfire throughout Europe, and all the royalty and people of quality just had to have one. It's a bit of a mystery why, since a picture of one from the 1500s shows a carriage with no roof and no suspension, but that's fashion for you! As the craze spread, so did the word describing it, coming into English from French as *coche* in the mid-1500s, and gradually applying to any conveyance. Its use in sports we owe to 19th-century English university students. In Oxonian in-group slang, a tutor who helped you get through your exams was a 'coach', because he carried or conveyed you along, sort of like a bus, geddit? Such wits they were. Since competitive rowing is a big thing at Oxford and Cambridge, this student slang term quickly came to apply to the person who helped train the rowing team, and from there spread to other sports.

UMPIRE

Originally (in the 14th century), the word was *noumpere*, from the Old French *nonper,* meaning not equal or not a pair, that is, a third party considered to be an impartial judge. *Noumpere* came into the language in the mid-1300s, but by the mid-1400s people had re-divided the word (in the same way they turned 'napron' into 'apron'), thinking that 'a noumpere' was actually 'an oumpere'. Thus the word lost its initial *n* and came down as 'umpire'. Originally it meant an arbitrator in a dispute. In sports its use dates from the 1700s.

SCOUT

Knowing that the word 'scout' was pronounced SKOOT in English before the Great Vowel Shift helps us to see its connection with the

Old French word *escouter*, which became the modern French word *écouter* meaning 'listen'. So the original meaning of the verb 'scout' in the 1300s was to be a spy, to travel around in search of information. The noun 'scout', which arose in the 1500s, meant the action of spying. Almost immediately it also meant the person doing the spying and reconnoitring for an army. The sports use dates from the early 20th century.

GYM

When the World Series is over, the players have to keep in shape till the opening of the Grapefruit League. To do this, many of them will spend time at the gym. This shortened form dates from the late 19th century. The longer form, 'gymnasium', comes via Latin from a Greek word *gymnazein* meaning 'exercise naked', from *gymnos* meaning 'naked'. (This is a handy tidbit of information to have to hand the next time someone tells you words should have only the meaning they had in Latin or Greek. Suggest that if they think that, then they should do their next workout starkers.) 'Gymnasium' entered the language in about 1600 in reference to Ancient Greek and Roman gymnasia. The first reference that is clearly to a modern gymnasium comes from about 1800, although 'gymnastic' and 'gymnastics' date from the 16th century. In fact our first quotation is from a 1574 publication improbably titled *Health Magazine*!

Diwali

&

The late-October or early-November Hindu festival honouring the goddess of prosperity, Lakshmi, is marked by the exchange of gifts and the lighting of lamps (indeed the name 'Diwali' comes from a word meaning 'a line of lamps'). A good opportunity to look at some of the words that have come into English from the languages of the Indian subcontinent.

SHAMPOO

'Shampoo' comes from a Hindi word *čampna* meaning 'to press'. When the English borrowed it in the 18th century, it meant 'to massage', so we have evidence, for instance, of a woman who would 'shampoo' her husband and then go and 'shampoo' the horse. The word came to mean 'apply detergent to the hair' in the mid-19th century (around about the time detergents came to be widespread); the substance used was called 'shampoo liquid' and then was shortened to 'shampoo'.

VERANDA

The word exists in many Indian languages, for instance Hindi (*varanda*) and Bengali (*baranda*), but the interesting thing is that the Indian languages seem to have borrowed it from Portuguese! The Portuguese had colonized Goa, on the west coast of India, from 1510 on; *varanda* is their word to designate a railing, balustrade, or balcony.

Round about 1700, when England was stuck in a period known as the Little Ice Age because of its cool temperatures, one can see that the English would have had little need for verandas, whereas it could be a very sensible addition to an Indian dwelling. Throughout the 18th century, mention is made of verandas only on buildings in India. Not until the 19th century do they appear on English houses.

BUNGALOW

In Hindi and Urdu *bangla* means 'belonging to Bengal'. Originally, a 'Bengali-style house' was a one-storey house of light construction, often with a thatched roof, for instance a summer house, many of which were constructed for the arriving Europeans. The word came to apply to houses in England only in the late 19th century. A particular Canadian usage of the word (which unwittingly harks back to its original sense in English) is found in Cape Breton, where 'bungalow' means 'summer cottage'.

TANK
In many Indian languages, a word similar to 'tank' designates a reservoir or cistern. In English, the word was first applied (in the 17th century) to man-made pools, lakes, or large cisterns used as reservoirs for storing water in India. Then by about 1700 the word came to apply to large receptacles for water (such as fish tanks) in England. But why are military armoured vehicles called 'tanks'? This came about because, in about December 1915, when the new weapon was being developed, 'tank' was used as a code word to maintain secrecy. It is not known why this particular word was chosen. Tanks were introduced on September 15, 1916, and described for a while as 'landships' ('which have been making such successful cruises on the sea of mud on the Somme', said the *Daily Mirror*), but 'tank' is the word that stuck.

DINGHY
In Hindi a *dingi* was a small rowboat in use on rivers in India. The English borrowed this in the early 19th century, and the word very quickly came to apply to a small boat as part of the equipment of a large ship. The *h* was added in English to distinguish the word from the adjective 'dingy'. Inflatable dinghies date from the Second World War.

BIG CHEESE
This expression has nothing to do with the dairy product. As we mentioned when talking about 'cream', 'cheese' was originally an

Anglo-Saxon word. But 'big cheese' comes from India. In Urdu the word *chiz* means 'thing'. Apparently, it used to be common among young Anglo-Indians in the early 19th century to speak of something that was highly commendable as 'the cheese' or 'the real cheese'. 'Big cheese' came to mean an important person in the 20th century.

REMEMBRANCE DAY

ॐ

Remembrance Day turns our thoughts to things military, including names of ranks, types of weapons, and even that thing denounced by wags as an oxymoron, 'military intelligence'.

SOLDIER
'Soldier' is actually related to 'solid'. Both words come from the Latin word *solidus*, which meant 'whole' or complete. A *solidus nummus* was a gold coin—literally a coin through and through. This got shortened to *solidus*, and borrowed into English via French as 'sold' (not the same 'sold' which is the past tense of 'sell') in the 1300s. In English it meant specifically the money paid to people in the army, who therefore became 'soldiers'.

LIEUTENANT
'Lieutenant' comes from the two French words *lieu* meaning 'place' and *tenant* meaning 'holding': literally a lieutenant is the person who would be holding his superior's place in the superior's absence. The really interesting question is, why do some people say LOOtenant and others LEFtenant? LOOtenant is closer to the Old French pronunciation, but right from our earliest evidence, in the

1300s and 1400s, we have spellings that indicate that both pronunciations existed. Probably the English had a hard time pronouncing French, or they may have confused *lieu* with the English
word they already knew, 'leave'. Or they confused the written *u*
with a *v*. For whatever reason, the 'loo-' version died out of British
English but survived in American English, and since Americans
were the founders of Canadian English when the Loyalists moved
here, we also inherited 'LOOtenant'. But the Canadian Forces have
always been strongly influenced by the British, so LEFtenant is the
official pronunciation there, even though, ironically, the Royal
Navy uses neither of these pronunciations but LETtenant instead.

COLONEL

Why is this word pronounced as if there were an *r* in it, even
though there isn't? English pronunciation must drive second-
language learners mad!

'Colonel' ultimately comes from Italian colonnello (from *colon-
na* meaning 'column'), meaning the commander of a company or
'column' of infantry. When the French borrowed this word, they
had a hard time saying 'colonel' with two *l*'s (though they manage
to do it now). So the first *l* got changed to an *r* and they ended up
with *coronel*, which is what got borrowed into English in the
1500s and then scrunched down to KERnel. In the 1600s people
looked at the origin of the word and changed the spelling back to
'colonel' to reflect the etymology, but the pronunciation stuck.

ADMIRAL

The word 'admiral' came into English from Arabic at the time of
the Crusades, in the 1200s, and at that time was used only to designate a Saracen ruler or commander. The Arabic word *amir*
meaning 'commander' has also given us 'emir' and 'emirate'. In
Arabic, *amir* was often followed by a phrase saying what the person was ruler *of*, so for instance *amir-al-bahr* meant 'ruler of the

sea', with *al* meaning 'the'. So Europeans thought that the word meaning 'ruler' was actually *amiral*. The Spanish and the Sicilians, who were most in touch with the Arabs, started calling the commanders of their own navies 'amiral of the sea'. This caught on with the Genoese, the French, and the English, and by 1500 the 'of the sea' had been dropped. 'Amiral' got confused with the Latin *admirare,* meaning 'to wonder at', and thus we ended up with 'admiral'.

DRAGOON

The word 'dragoon' survives in names of armoured regiments like the Royal Canadian Dragoons. The armoured regiments, who now drive around in tanks, were originally cavalry regiments, and dragoons were no exception. They were mounted soldiers who were armed with a musket, also called a dragoon, or in French, a *dragon*. There are three possible explanations why this gun was called a dragoon. One theory is that it 'breathed fire' like a dragon. Another is that the hammer on the gun looked like a dragon's head. And finally it could just be that the soldiers were united under a military banner also called a 'dragon' because originally a dragon was depicted on it (think of the Welsh flag, for instance).

Dragoons were originally a kind of downmarket cavalry, rabble mounted on old nags and beasts of burden. They were notorious for robbing and pillaging, tasks made easier because their horses provided a getaway vehicle. Louis XIV persecuted the Huguenots by billeting dragoons on them, and from this came our use of the verb 'dragoon' meaning to coerce by force or harassment.

KHAKI

'Khaki' is a fascinating word that comes from an Urdu word meaning 'dust'. The colour, probably achieved by washing the fabric in muddy water, was adopted for use in uniforms by the British army in India and Afghanistan in the 1840s, the first use of camouflage (if you think of the pictures we see of Afghanistan on TV, you can see why khaki is good camouflage). Up till then, of course, the British wore highly conspicuous red uniforms, but with improvements in the accuracy of firearms, the wisdom of camouflage became obvious. An interesting thing about 'khaki' is that some, especially older, Canadians have a unique pronunciation of it: KARkee.

CAMOUFLAGE

Although the idea of camouflage dates from the 1840s, the word 'camouflage' itself was not used until the First World War. The French used it in 1914, and the English had adopted it by 1917. In French the verb *camoufler* had existed since the early 19th century, meaning 'disguise'. There are two possibilities to explain how the French got it. One is that they borrowed it as a slang term from an Italian word *camuffare*, meaning 'disguise'; *camuffare* came from an old Italian word, *camuffo,* for a hood worn to conceal the face, which was subsequently used to mean 'a thief'. The other possibility is that it is derived from another French word, *camouflet*, which designated a trick consisting of blowing smoke in someone's face while they were sleeping. Why the French needed a word for this activity is lost in the mists of time.

BOMB

A bomb is literally something that goes 'boom', since the word comes ultimately from a Greek word *bombos*, designating a booming or humming noise. The word was first applied, in the late 17th century, to what today would be called a 'shell' (a projectile from a mortar), presumably because shells make a humming noise while whizzing through the air.

ROCKET

'Rocket' came into English from Italian in the early 1600s. The

Italian word *rochetta* meant a small distaff (a distaff being the cleft stick on which wool is wound before spinning by hand), and the cylindrical rocket was similar in shape.

MISSILE

'Missile' comes from the same Latin word meaning 'to send' which has also given us 'mission' and 'missive'. When it first appeared in English, about 1600, 'missile' was used to mean gifts, such as sweets and perfumes, thrown by Roman emperors to crowds as largesse. So our first quotation, in a translation of Suetonius, is the retrospectively hilarious: 'Scattered also abroad there were for the people Missils, during the whole time of those Plaies.' By the 1650s, though, the word was being used of weapons rather than gifts.

WEAPONS OF MASS DESTRUCTION

Ever since war became another kind of 'reality TV' with the Gulf War of 1991, we have seen how the mass media can almost instantly promote a word from the status of military jargon or slang to common parlance. This tendency has only increased with the most recent war in Iraq. The words that strike us as 'brand new', however, may only be, to use the euphemism of second-hand-car dealers, 'new to you'. We think of 'weapons of mass destruction', for instance, as a very new term, but in fact we have evidence for it dating back to 1937. Because it is a bit of a mouthful, we have started to substitute the much snappier 'WMDs', which, like all acronyms, also has the advantage of distancing us from the unpleasant meaning of the words.

WEAPONIZE

This word has been much vilified as a nasty neologism. I am not sure why self-appointed 'language commentators' reserve such vitriol for words ending in the very convenient (and very ancient) suffix '-ize', but they have apparently been complaining about it since at least 1594, according to the OED. 'Weaponize', no matter how new it may seem, is now well into middle age, having been in use since at least 1956.

REGIME CHANGE
How innocent and non-violent 'regime change' sounds, rather like the changing of the guard. Certainly no 2,000-pound bombs involved. And indeed, our first evidence for 'regime change', from 1965, simply refers to the replacement of one government by another. But 'regime' has had increasingly derogatory connotations ever since it entered English at the time of the French Revolution when it referred to the *ancien régime*. A 'regime' is almost by definition now something nasty, and one supposes that the users of this word hope listeners will acquiesce in the thought that changing it (by whatever means) is A Good Thing.

SUICIDE BOMBER
This is a word I am sure we wish we were not so familiar with. We feel that it cropped up out of nowhere in the mid-1990s, but in fact the term was being used to designate kamikaze pilots as early as 1941.

CASUALTY
Much is made in every war of the tendency to use new euphemisms ('friendly fire' and 'collateral damage' were the big euphemisms of the 1991 Gulf War) to disguise the horrific realities of armed conflict. Before we condemn the current mouthpieces of the military for being more weasely than their forebears, however, we would do well to consider the word 'casualty', which simply meant 'a chance occurrence' when it entered the language in the 1400s. Over the course of 400 years it travelled a downward path from 'accident' to 'bad accident' to

'accident causing injury' to 'wounded person' to 'death'. The Duke of Wellington referred to 'casualties' in the Napoleonic Wars. No doubt the Iron Duke would acquit himself very well at a Pentagon briefing!

CONSPIRE, CONSPIRACY

'Conspire' comes from a Latin word meaning literally 'breathe together' (from *con* 'together' and *spirare* 'breathe'), but figuratively 'to agree or be united in a purpose'. Already in Latin the word had acquired the sinister meaning of plotting to do something evil.

CODE

'Code' comes ultimately from a word meaning a tree trunk. This was the Latin *caudex*, which was later changed to *codex*. From meaning the trunk of a tree, *codex* came to mean a wooden tablet on which something was carved, then a book rather than a scroll, and finally a code of laws. From the idea of a sophisticated categorization of something came, first, the idea of a systematized set of symbols for military communication, and ultimately a set of numbers, letters, or symbols for identifying something.

CIPHER

'Cipher' is the oldest word in English for 'zero', predating 'nought' and 'zero' itself by a good 200 years. It is derived from an Arabic word meaning 'empty' and first appears in English in 1399. Before that, there was no word for zero, because Europeans used Roman numerals and *had* no zero. Just as we owe the word 'cipher' to the Arabs, who were the mathematical whizzes of the early Middle Ages, to them we owe, like so many other mathematical discoveries, our whole numbering system, which we still call 'Arabic'. Arabic numerals started being introduced to Europe in the 1200s, but they were objects of fear and superstition for a long time, perceived as some sort of arcane knowledge probably connected with the occult. What's more, they were just hard to understand for someone brought up on Roman numerals. In particular the whole notion of zeroes, or ciphers, was hard for people to get their head around. So 'cipher' also came to be used to mean a set of secret symbols to hide the meaning of something, hence its use to mean 'code'.

Eventually, people did realize how useful Arabic numerals were, especially because trade was booming in 14th-century Europe and merchants needed a less cumbersome method of calculating than Roman numerals. But the thing that really assured the success of the zero was the invention of double-entry bookkeeping by the Italians sometime before 1340. Without the zero, you couldn't balance your credits and debits, so Arabic numerals were bound to win out.

SABOTAGE

There is a folk etymology running around that this word has its origins in French textile workers throwing their wooden clogs (*sabots*) into mechanized looms in fits of Luddite petulance. I can find absolutely no support for this theory. Another explanation dates the word from a French railway strike in 1910, when the strikers cut the *sabots*, or wooden shoes that held the rails in place. It is true that the first use of 'sabotage' in English dates from this railway strike, but its use in French goes back a few decades before that. It seems that *sabotage* is just an extension of a sense that the word *saboter* already had in French, which was 'perform work badly, clumsily, or carelessly'. Indeed, in English we could talk about doing work in a 'slipshod' manner. So we see that both English and French use words designating a kind of footwear to refer to careless work. Also, when you think of it, the word 'clog' in English means both a wooden shoe and an obstruction. So the theory about the workers literally sabotaging things with their shoes, though picturesque, is unfounded.

CLOAK AND DAGGER

This expression has its origins in a Spanish theatrical genre popular in the 17th century. This was called the *comedia de capa y espada*, or literally the 'cape and sword drama'. The plays were typically full of intrigue, adventure, and melodrama, and the characters were invariably from the upper middle classes, who wore short capes and swords. We don't really know why 'cloak and sword' got changed to 'cloak and dagger' in English, though obviously a dagger is easier to conceal than a sword if you're up to some skulduggery. 'Cloak' itself comes from the French word *cloche*, for 'bell', because of its shape.

COMPANY

'The Company' is a well-known nickname for the CIA. 'Company' and 'companion' come from the Latin words *cum* meaning 'with' and *panis* meaning 'bread', so literally your companion is the person you break bread with.

SNOOP

'Snoop' comes from a Dutch word meaning to eat something on the sly or, as the OED puts it, 'appropriate and consume dainties in a clandestine manner'. (We have to assume the OED was thinking of the food sense of dainties and not the ladies' frilly underwear sense!) Like so many Dutch words, it came into English via the US in the 1800s.

GROUND TRUTH

At Pentagon briefings, when journalists ask inconvenient questions about whose missile it was that wiped out a street market, the briefers say they are waiting for 'ground truth'. Although one might be tempted to think that this is truth that has been pulverized until unrecognizable as such, the term actually originated in remote sensing in the sixties. It designated information obtained by direct measurement at ground level as opposed to that acquired by aerial or satellite images. It has gradually extended its meaning to 'information that has been checked at source'.

Sale! Hurry in!

ॐ

Hardly is Remembrance Day over before our mailboxes start overflowing with flyers advertising wares that we are expected to buy for Christmas. It is the hottest retail season of the year, so time to look at words having to do with selling, buying, and that all-important commodity, money.

ADVERTISING
The word 'advertise' comes ultimately from Latin *advertere,* which meant 'to turn towards' (*vertere* means 'to turn') and more specifically to turn someone's attention to something, especially as a warning or admonition. When 'advertise' entered English in the 15th century, it did in fact mean 'warn', as *avertir* does to this day in French. But before long it lost its ominous overtones and came to mean simply 'call attention to' or 'point out', especially to the general public. By the 1700s it came to mean specifically making something publicly known by a published announcement. Nowadays such 'announcements' usually have the purpose of selling something.

PROPAGANDA
'Propaganda' comes to us from Church Latin. In 1622, Pope Gregory XV established a committee of cardinals to be in charge of

foreign missions, coinciding with the upsurge of European colonization. This committee was called the 'Congregation for the Propagation of the Faith', but of course its actual name wasn't English but Latin, the *Congregatio de propaganda fide*. The full name was a bit of a mouthful, both in Latin and in English, so it got shortened to 'the propaganda'. Soon other people cottoned on to the idea of having associations or concerted plans to promote some doctrine or practice, and 'propaganda' came to mean usually a political group promoting subversive ideas. By the mid-19th century, the word was being used to mean biased information systematically disseminated in order to promote a particular political cause. The first use of the phrase 'propaganda war' was in reference to the Napoleonic wars.

BUMF

All this hype and puffery can be dismissed collectively as 'bumf'. 'Bumf' was late-19th-century schoolboy slang, a shortening of 'bum-fodder', meaning toilet paper. 'Bum-fodder' had been around in this sense since a 17th-century translation of Rabelais, but in 1753 we find it, surprisingly, in the metaphorical sense of useless printed material in the title of a magazine article: 'Bum fodder for the ladies'. Unfortunately we have no further information about that magazine article! 'Bumf' naturally went through the same evolution as 'bum-fodder' very quickly. This is a word that is used in Britain a lot and also in Canada, but not in the US.

PAMPHLET

'Pamphlet' has its origins in a 12th-century Latin love poem, surprisingly. The hero of the poem was called Pamphilus, and the story, a very popular erotic comedy in the 1200s, came to be known as *The Pamphilet*. It was so popular that the students at the University of Paris were rebuked because, as the OED puts it, 'they preferred this erotic production to more edifying reading'. It was a fairly short piece which was widely distributed, and by the early 1400s the word 'pamfilet' or 'pamflet' was being used to mean any short text with fewer pages than a book, usually unbound, and usually of a more serious nature than the original *Pamphilet*!

BROCHURE

This comes to us from French, where it literally means 'a stitched work', from *brocher* meaning 'to stitch', which ultimately comes from Latin *brocca* meaning a spike. Obviously the few sheets of paper forming a brochure were originally simply stitched together with thread, though now they are stapled. But if you go to a printer, you will find that this kind of stapling is still called 'saddlestitching'.

HUCKSTER

'Huckster' is quite an old word, going back to about 1300, when it meant someone who sold items at a market stall. It probably comes from a Germanic word meaning 'haggle'. By the 1500s it came to have derogatory connotations, being used for someone who hoarded food to profiteer by selling it later at a higher price, someone who sold fraudulently, or someone ready to profit from any transaction no matter how dishonest or unethical. Its use for someone involved in advertising dates from the 1940s.

PUBLICITY

'Publicity' obviously comes from 'public', which is actually a confusion of two Latin words. The first was *poplicus* from *populus*, meaning 'of the people'. *Poplicus* was changed in Latin to *publicus* under the influence of *pubes*, which meant 'adult men' or 'the male population'. Now, *pubes* has also, of course, given us 'pubescent' and 'puberty' and 'pubic', because in Latin the word was used to mean 'adult' but also to designate the pubic hair, presumably because it is a sign of adulthood. So publicity and pubic hair are etymologically related, a fact that few publicists wish to be reminded of, I'm sure.

MONEY, MINT

The ancient Romans had a goddess called Moneta (which meant 'she who warns'), who was either a goddess in her own right or possibly just another name for Juno, the wife of Jupiter. In any case, the temple of Moneta or Juno Moneta was used as a place to coin money, so *moneta* in Latin came to mean a mint, and from there to mean coins made in the mint, and subsequently to mean money in general. The word *moneta* passed into Old French as *moneie*, the *t* having disappeared, which very commonly happened going from Latin to French. From France, of course, it came over to England with the Normans. In modern French, *monnaie* still means coins or change rather than money.

Meanwhile, however, back in about the 3rd century, while the Gallo-Romans were doing their best to corrupt the word *moneta* into *moneya*, the Germanic tribes whom the Romans had conquered were also working their own particular phonetic transformations on the word *moneta*. Unlike the French, they tended to keep the consonants and drop the vowels, so when the Angles and Saxons came over to Britain in the 5th century, they already had a word derived from *moneta*: *mynet*, meaning 'coin'. In the 15th century, the word, now reduced to *mynt*, was applied to the place where coins are produced. Meanwhile, it ceased to be used to mean 'a metal piece of money', because that job had been taken over by 'coin'.

COIN

If you look at the English word 'coin', it is identical to the French word *coin* meaning 'corner', but the words seem totally unrelated. In fact, they are one and the same word, because the original dies for stamping money were wedge-shaped, or 'corner-shaped', one might say. These were therefore called *coignes*, and by Chaucer's time the word was also applied to the metal disks stamped with these dies.

ENTREPRENEUR

In French, *entrepreneur* means 'a person who undertakes something'. The word had come into English briefly from French in the form of 'entreprenour' in the 1400s, at which time it meant a champion in a battle. But it quickly died out and was borrowed in its modern form only in the early 19th century. But at that time it was used only for someone who organized or conducted musical entertainments—what we could call an impresario, probably (*impresario* being the Italian word meaning 'one who undertakes'). By the mid-19th century, however, it had come to have its present meaning of a person who engages in a business at their own risk.

TYCOON

Originally a Japanese word derived from Chinese *ta* 'great' and *kiun* 'prince', this was used as an honorific title meaning 'great ruler' for the shoguns, or military generals, who ruled Japan until the late 19th century. Shortly after relations between Japan and the US were opened up in the 1850s, the word was used as a nickname for Abraham Lincoln. Then it was used jocularly to mean any sort of head honcho (a word we have also borrowed from Japanese, meaning 'group leader') until by the end of the 19th century, when American industrialists were making vast fortunes and wielding considerable political influence, and were comparable in power and wealth to the Japanese shoguns, 'tycoon' was used to mean a wealthy businessman.

MONEYBAGS

With the Industrial Revolution in full swing and the Empire

expanding, 19th-century England was also a good place for entrepreneurs and tycoons, and it's interesting to note that our first evidence of the word 'moneybags' to mean 'a wealthy person' dates from the early 19th century. The source, however, is quite surprising: it's found in a poem by John Keats!

TRADE

'Trade' is actually related to the word 'tread'. It originally meant a path or course trodden by a person, and then by extension the track or course followed by a ship. We got it in the 14th century from Hanseatic German, which is not surprising, because this was the time when the Hanseatic League of northern German cities dominated European commerce. So you would talk about the 'trade' followed by a ship going from Hamburg to England. And since ships would ply back and forth habitually on the same course, 'trade' soon came to mean a regular or habitual course of action. This is why we talk about 'trade winds', which are winds that blow habitually in the same direction. The fact that they were conducive to what we now understand by the word 'trade' between England and the West Indies is coincidental. So 'trade' came also to mean one's habitual occupation, and particularly the occupation of buying and selling, which before had been called 'merchandise'.

BEYOND THE ADVENT CALENDAR

&

The end of November or beginning of December brings us to the beginning of Advent, four weeks in which to focus either on the imminent birth of Christ or on the thrill of eating a new chocolate every day, depending on one's inclinations. This gives us an opportunity to look at words that have their origins in Christianity.

ADVENT

'Advent' is a fairly simple word derived from the Latin *adventus* meaning arrival. Its earliest use in English, from about the year 1000, was to designate the liturgical season leading up to Christmas, the 'arrival' of Christ on earth. And it meant only this for a good 700 or 800 years. It wasn't until about the Victorian era that it started being used to mean some other notable arrival. I wonder what people from the Middle Ages would make of reading sentences like 'the advent of vacuum cleaners' or 'the advent of automated teller machines'!

CRETIN

The story behind 'cretin' is actually quite touching. Now, the cretinism we're talking about here is a specific type of mental retardation and deformation, and not just using 'cretin' as a catchall term of abuse for someone you consider stupid. This medical condition is caused by a lack of thyroid hormone in an unborn or newborn child. This is often caused by insufficient iodine in the diet, and, back in the days before iodized salt, it was a particular problem in landlocked parts of Europe where people didn't have access to fish from the sea, which was the only source of iodine. So cretinism was quite common in the Swiss and French Alps. In the French dialect of that area, *cretin* was a variant of *chrétien*, meaning Christian, and was applied to these sorely afflicted individuals, the idea being to remind people that cretins were human beings with souls just like everyone else.

MAUDLIN

'Maudlin' is a corruption of the name of St Mary Magdalen.

Indeed, 'Magdalen' was pronounced and often spelled Maudlin in the Middle Ages, which explains why there is a college in Oxford spelled Magdalen but pronounced Maudlin by all but the unwary tourists! Now, Mary Magdalen, who is mentioned by name in the Gospels only as a follower of Christ who watched at the Crucifixion, was often identified in tradition with the unnamed 'sinner' in Luke's gospel who came to see Jesus, wept, and then bathed his feet with her tears and dried them with her long hair. As a result, in art Mary Magdalen was often depicted as weeping, either in this particular incident or by the cross. So by 1600 'maudlin' was being used to mean 'weepy', and particularly to designate any effusive display of sentimentality, especially by someone who is drunk.

PETREL

The word 'petrel' we owe to another saint and another Gospel story. Petrels are a type of seabird that fly far from land and have the habit of flying low over the water with their legs dangling so that they look as though they are walking on the water. They were therefore named after St Peter, because in the famous Bible story where Jesus comes walking toward the disciples on the Sea of Galilee, Peter jumps out of the boat and starts walking towards him on the water.

TALENT

'Talent' comes to us from yet another Gospel story, a parable in fact. A talent was a kind of money in the ancient world, the name deriving from a Greek word meaning 'scales', because it designated a certain weight of silver or gold. In the famous parable in St Matthew's Gospel, a master gives his slaves a number of talents to look after for him while he is away. Two of them make money with their capital but the third just digs a hole in the ground and puts his talent in there for safekeeping. As punishment for not making good enough use of his talent, he is thrown into the outer darkness, where there is weeping and wailing and gnashing of teeth. Now of course this is all allegorical and not a Biblical endorsement of entrepreneurialism, so in the late Middle Ages, 'talent' took on a new meaning of the powers or abilities that a person may be naturally endowed with, seen as divinely entrusted to them to use well. By the 1600s the idea of a talent being a gift from God with an obligation attached to it was weaker, and talent came to mean simply a natural ability of any kind, no matter what use you put it to.

SHORT SHRIFT
Shrift was an Old English word meaning confession to a priest and the receiving of a penance and absolution. A short shrift was a brief space of time allowed to a criminal to make his confession and receive absolution before being executed. From this it acquired its current meaning of rapid and unsympathetic dismissal.

CONSIGN
'Consign' originally meant 'mark with the sign of the cross'. So tracing the sign of the cross on a baby's head at baptism was 'consigning'. Subsequently, 'consign' came to mean mark with any sign, such as your family seal. When you handed over a possession formally, you would have to mark it with your seal or signature, so that became known as consigning something to someone. And very quickly 'consign' came to have the meaning of putting something or someone somewhere to be rid of them.

PATTER
This isn't the patter of rain on a roof or the pitter-patter of little feet, but patter as in a salesman's spiel. It comes from *Pater Noster*, the first words ('Our Father') of the Lord's Prayer in Latin.

Now as anyone knows who has said the same memorized prayers over and over again, it is very easy to lapse into doing it in a mechanical, rapid, or mumbling way. People weren't any different back in the Middle Ages, so 'patter' originally meant muttering the Lord's prayer (and subsequently any prayer) fast, without paying much attention to it. From those origins 'patter' came to mean any smooth, rapid, or glib talk that pays little attention to meaning.

CAPPUCCINO
In Italian, *cappuccino* literally means a Capuchin monk. Capuchins are Franciscan monks who got their name because their habit included a sharp pointed hood, or *cappuccio* in Italian. And, being Franciscans, their habit is brown, much like the colour of... cappuccino! Capuchin monkeys are also named after Capuchin monks, because they (the monkeys that is) have caps of hair on their heads that looks like a monk's cowl.

ONLY 24 SHOPPING DAYS LEFT

හ

December is devoted to frantic Christmas shopping. This hectic and overwhelming activity, rushing from one shop or boutique to another, can seem like anything but 'retail therapy'.

MALL
Heading to the mall before Christmas may seem like an endurance sport, and 'mall' does have its origin in sports. It was originally, in the 1600s, a long alley in which the game of pall-

mall was played. The object of pall-mall was to whack a wooden ball with a mallet through a suspended iron ring at the end of one of these long alleys in as few strokes as possible. It was sort of like croquet combined with basketball, I suppose. The name came from Italian *pallamaglio*, with *palla* meaning 'ball' and *maglio* meaning 'mallet', derived from the Latin word for hammer, *malleus*, which has also given us 'malleable' (which literally means something that can easily be hammered). The alley which came to be known as a mall was quite long: the one still called 'The Mall' in St James's Park in London is eight hundred yards long. The Mall became a very fashionable promenade in the 17th and 18th centuries, presumably after the game fell from favour, because otherwise fashionable promenaders would have been beaned.

Soon every fashionable city had to have its own promenade called a mall. Since many of these 'malls' were sheltered in some way (promenading in the English climate being a risky proposition), when enclosed shopping centres were invented in the fifties the word 'mall' seemed appropriate for the long, wide, covered walkway down the middle, and thus for the entire shopping complex.

HECTIC

Christmas shopping can certainly be hectic. The word actually comes from a Greek word *hektikos* meaning 'habitual', which I guess is appropriate for mall crawlers anyway. Indeed, at this time of the year they seem to be habitually frantic. Now, I don't think the Greeks were into Christmas shopping, so they used 'hectic' to apply to diseases which were habitually accompanied by a fever, especially consumption, and that is how it entered English in the late 1300s. 'Hectic' went along in English for about five hundred years meaning, literally, 'habitually feverish'. It wasn't until the beginning of the 20th century that it was used to mean, figuratively, 'characterized by a state of feverish activity or excitement'.

OVERWHELM

'Overwhelm' comes from two words: 'over' and 'whelm'. That's not a very informative word history, because 'whelm' is a verb that is not used by itself anymore, but it did indeed exist in the Middle Ages. 'Whelm' meant, literally, 'to capsize or overturn' or simply to turn upside down. So you could whelm your teacup on your saucer if you wanted to. 'Overwhelm' was just a more forceful version of this, and since it meant 'capsize' it also was understood to describe the action of the water after it had capsized your boat— covering it over and submerging it—so that's where this idea of drowning people in things came up. It was a handy word to use figuratively of troubles overwhelming you or work overwhelming you or debts overwhelming you or Christmas shopping drowning people, so to speak.

RETAIL

'Retail' comes from the Old French verb *retaillier,* which meant 'to cut again'. The literal idea was that the merchant would get a huge hunk of cheese or something wholesale and cut smaller bits off it to sell retail. The root verb in *retaillier* is also found in the word 'tailor', literally a 'cutter' of clothes.

BOUTIQUE

'Boutique' comes to us from the same Greek word that gave us 'apothecary'. *Apotheke* in Greek simply meant 'a storehouse'; it came from a word that meant 'to lay away, to store'. So an apothecary was originally simply a store, and specifically a store that sold non-perishable goods like herbs and spices. Of course, because herbs were the medieval equivalent of prescription drugs, the apothecary was effectively the drugstore. That's how the word 'apothecary' became restricted to the selling of drugs. But meanwhile *apotheke* in Greek (meaning any kind of store) had also migrated into French where, under the influence of a Provençal word, it was changed to *boutique*. The English quite happily borrowed this in the 1700s (when it was very trendy to borrow French words) to designate a specialty shop of some sort.

WINTER

WASSAIL, WASSAIL
ALL OVER THE TOWN

&

The shopping is done, the presents are wrapped, and all that is left to do is to sit back, enjoy the holidays, and eat a lot of rich food.

HOLIDAY

In Old English, the word we know today as 'holy' was *halig*, pronounced 'hally'. A saint's day or other church festival (when, of course, everyone had the day off work) was therefore a 'hally day' or 'holy day'. In the Middle Ages, the pronunciation of 'holy' started to shift from 'hally' to 'holly', with both 'halliday' and 'holiday' surviving side by side until the 1500s, when 'holiday' won out. We still hear remnants of this pronunciation variation in the way people pronounce 'Halloween': some say 'HAL' and others 'HOL'. The 'halliday' form of 'holiday' has survived, however, in the family name 'Halliday' originally given to people born on a holy day. In the 1500s, the 'holly' pronunciation shifted again, leaving us with the present-day 'holy', but the older pronunciation remained in the word 'holiday'.

YULE

'Yule' comes from an Anglo-Saxon word (which in turn came from Norse) which predates the Latinate word 'Christmas' (literally 'Christ's mass'). 'Yule' meant December or January, in particular a pre-Christian feast lasting twelve days. This probably accounts for the 'twelve days of Christmas' from December 25th to Epiphany on January 6th. Yule logs burning throughout the festival were a symbol of perpetual light. The name of the pagan festival was later applied to Christmas after the conversion of the Anglo-Saxons, much as the word for a pagan festival, Easter, was applied to the feast of the Resurrection.

WASSAIL

'Wassail' started out as a formula of greeting in Old English and Old Norse, *wes hál,* meaning 'be in good health'. It came from *wes*, the imperative of the verb 'to be' (which was even more irregular then than now), and *hál*, which meant 'healthy' (and still survives in 'hale and hearty'). *Wes hál* developed into a drinking formula thanks to the Danes living in the North of England and spread throughout England. After the Normans invaded England in 1066, 'wassail' was a word that they considered to be markedly characteristic of Englishmen, rather perhaps as Americans consider 'eh' to be characteristic of Canadians. One Anglo-Norman author even attributed the defeat of the English at the battle of Hastings to their having spent too much time the night before in drunken carousing, with abundant cries of 'wassail!' So 'wassail' was the 'cheers' of the Middle Ages. By about 1300, the word was also being applied to the drinks themselves, especially the spiced ale drunk at Christmas Eve and Twelfth Night celebrations. 'Wassail' would probably have died out altogether but it was one of those archaisms that Walter Scott popularized.

REINDEER

Now, one might think, with visions of Donner and Blitzen and Co. harnessed up to Santa's sleigh in our heads, that reindeer are so called because they wear reins. But the reins used for horses are derived from the Latin word *retinere*, which has also given us 'retain', whereas 'reindeer' comes from Old Norse. In fact, *rein* in Old Norse was the name for that particular type of deer, what we would call a caribou. This leaves us wondering, if *rein* already meant 'reindeer', why they needed to call it a 'reindeer deer', but 'deer' didn't specifically mean a cervid back then; it meant simply 'animal', just like the modern German word *Tier* (pronounced TEER). To Canadianize things a bit, the two elements of *rein* and *deer* meant 'caribou animal'.

CHOCOLATE

If St Nick is lucky, he may find a steaming mug of hot chocolate with miniature marshmallows waiting for him. (Actually, when I was a child, my father assured me that what Santa *really* liked was beer, and sure enough the beer that was left out was always drained to the last drop.) 'Chocolate' (both the word and the thing) came to England from Spain at the beginning of the 1600s, but the Spanish had found it in Mexico, where the Aztecs drank a concoction of cacao dissolved in water with sapodilla kernels and corn which they called *chocolatl*. This may have been a combination of a Maya word for 'hot', *chocol*, and a Nahuatl (the language of the Aztecs) word for 'water', *atl*.

An active ingredient in chocolate is 'theobromine'. Imagine offering a box of theobromines to your sweetheart! This frightfully scientific-sounding word actually has a delightful etymology. When the Swedish botanist Carolus Linnaeus was classifying the plant system in the 1700s, he had to think up a name for the genus of the cacao tree. Being a chocolate lover, he called it *Theobroma*, from the Greek *theo* meaning 'god' and *broma* meaning 'food': the food of the gods.

MINIATURE

One would think that this has something to do with 'minute' or 'mini'. But one would be wrong! The real story is much more surprising. The word comes from the Latin *minium* meaning 'red lead', a bright red oxide of lead formerly used in artists' paints. In the Middle Ages, the scribes used this pigment in their illuminated manuscripts, especially for titles, headings, and initials. A verb, *miniare*, was derived in Italian from *minium*, meaning to illuminate a manuscript, and a *miniatura* was an illumination in a manuscript, in any variety of colours. Since these illustrations were necessarily very small, 'miniature', which English borrowed from Italian, came to mean any small picture, and subsequently any small thing, including marshmallows.

NICKNAME

Since we're talking about St Nick, let's take a little diversion to explore the word 'nickname'. In fact, it has nothing to do with the name 'Nick', but it's too interesting to leave out. The original word in the 1300s was 'eke-name', from the Anglo-Saxon word *eke* meaning 'also'. An 'eke-name' was an 'also-name', a name in addition to your real one. Since *eke* gradually died out of the language, people didn't recognize it as an element and began to think that 'an eke-name' was actually 'a neke-name'. The *n* migrated from the end of 'an' and affixed itself to the beginning of the noun, where it stuck, leaving us with 'nickname'.

ORANGE

Something similar happened with the word 'orange'—that traditional offering left by Santa in the toe of our Christmas stocking—but in reverse. 'Orange' is derived from an Arabic word *naranj* (ultimately from a Sanskrit word, *naranga*). The fruit was introduced by the Arabs into Sicily in the Middle Ages and from there into France. Both the Italians and the French thought that there were just too many darned *n*'s in *una narancia* or *une narange*, so they dropped the initial *n* and assimilated it to the article. Then the French continued to meddle with the word, changing the initial (by that point) *a* into an *o* by analogy with the name of the Provençal town Orange, which derived its name from Arausio, a Gaulish god, but coincidentally was a centre for orange-growing. The spelling may also have been influenced by the French word for 'gold', *or*. By the time the English got hold of the word sometime in the 14th century, the initial *n* was long gone. The oranges in question were the bitter ones we now call Seville oranges, and they probably were not all that common in England. The sweet oranges weren't introduced to Europe until the 16th century.

'Orange' was first used of a colour in the early 1500s. This leads one to the question, what word did people use to designate the colour we know as orange before we had the word 'orange'? We have evidence of 'saffron' used as a colour in the late 1300s, but what did they do before that? Well, it seems there simply wasn't a word. People would have had to use either 'red' or 'yellow' depending on what shade of orange they were looking at.

MANDARIN

A type of orange which comes into season just in time for stocking stuffing is the mandarin. The word is related to the word 'mantra': both are ultimately derived from the Sanskrit *man,* meaning 'to think'. The Chinese officials called mandarins were supposed to be wise counsellors who thought a lot. The oranges are probably so called in reference to the yellow-orange garments worn by the Chinese officials. The variety of Chinese known as Mandarin is so called because it was spoken by the educated and ruling classes. Civil servants have been called 'mandarins' since the early 20th century; whether they are wise counsellors who think a lot I will leave to you to decide.

CANDY

Next up in the stocking is the candy. This word comes to us from the French *sucre candi*, in which *candi* was not a noun, but an adjective describing a type of sugar that has been clarified and turned into large crystals by repeated boiling and evaporation. The French borrowed the term *candi* from the Arabs, who in turn got it from Persian; it goes back ultimately to a Sanskrit word meaning 'break into pieces', because the 'sugar candy' was in large chunks.

WALNUT
You might also find in your stocking some whole, unshelled walnuts, which are not, as you might surmise, nuts that grow by walls. 'Walnut' comes from the Old English *wealh-hnutu,* which meant literally 'foreign nut', because the tree was not native to England (and indeed was not imported there by the French till the 15th century). The first element of the word is also the root for the name of Wales, because when the Anglo-Saxons arrived in Britain in the 5th century, they considered the Welsh (Celts who had been living in the British Isles for centuries) to be 'foreigners'. Pretty arrogant of them, really!

TINSEL
After ransacking the stocking, it's time to hit the tree for presents, admiring the tree-trimming in passing. 'Tinsel' comes from the French *étincelle*, meaning 'spark'. This in turn came from the Latin *scintilla*, which has also given us 'scintillating'. In the early 1500s, 'tinsel' was a kind of fabric interwoven with metallic thread or decorated with spangles. By about 1600, the word was being used of spangles or strips of metallic material used in cheap and showy ornamentation and gaudy stage costumes. The specific Christmas-tree-decoration sense dates only from the 20th century.

PERFUME
A popular present, perfume. Perhaps it would be less popular if people knew that the word is related to 'fume'. Originally, in the 1500s, 'perfume' meant 'to perfuse with smoke'—to fumigate, in fact. Try offering your loved one a fumigation for Christmas! Perfume was originally a substance burned to give off a sweet smell,

like incense, and more specifically the word applied to the scented smoke and fumes given off by the burning substance. It soon came to mean any sweet smell, or the scented liquid worn on the body.

SCENT

'Scent' was originally used as a verb, in the sense of hunting dogs detecting their prey by smell. It came from the Latin word *sentire*, meaning to feel or perceive. The verb was used as a noun meaning, first, the dog's sense of smell and then the odour of the prey. It was not until a good four hundred years later, in the 18th century, that the word came to be used for a sweet-smelling perfume. No one knows why 'scent' is spelled with a *c*; for the first three or four hundred years of its life it was spelled 'sent', but then all of a sudden the *c* was inserted in the 1700s.

EGGNOG

With the presents opened, the hours waiting for the turkey to be cooked can be passed with a glass or two of eggnog. What is a nog? In the late 17th century, we start seeing the word used for a type of ale made in East Anglia (the bulgy bit of eastern England north of the Thames Estuary). Where 'nog' came from is uncertain. It may be related to 'noggin', which designated a small drinking vessel in the 1500s, two hundred years before boxers started using it as slang for 'head'. In the 19th century, someone had the bright idea of concocting a drink consisting of heated beer, cider, wine, or other liquor with, if you can imagine it, an egg whisked in. This they called an 'egg-nog'. The recipe has, thankfully, changed since then but still contains eggs and usually alcohol.

DAINTIES

An assortment of small cakes and cookies, especially small squares like Nanaimo bars, brownies, maybe some gingerbread cookies, and so on, may be waiting on the coffee table to accompany your eggnog. In western Canada, it is common to call these collectively 'dainties'. Be warned, you prairie folk: in my experience, if you mention 'dainties' to Ontarians, they think you're talking about ladies' underwear! 'Dainty' is actually related to the word 'dignity', for it is derived from the same Latin root, *dignitatem*. It came through Old French, which explains why it lost a syllable from the Latin word, as *daintié*. For the French in about 1200, the word could indeed be used to mean 'a tasty morsel', but more particularly it was applied to deer testicles. A bit of a long way from Nanaimo bars! When 'dainty' was first used in English in the 13th century, it was as a noun meaning 'esteem' or 'affectionate regard'. The word then went through several rapid shifts of meaning, to 'affection', 'liking for doing something', 'pleasure taken in doing something', 'a delightful thing', and 'a delicacy', which last sense it already had in 1300. 'Dainty' became an adjective later, in the mid-1300s, originally meaning 'excellent', then 'pleasing to the taste', then 'delicately beautiful'.

GINGERBREAD

Gingerbread does have something to do with ginger, but nothing to do with bread. It comes from a medieval Latin word *gingibratum,* meaning preserved ginger, which in Old French became *gingimbrat*. In about 1300, English had a word spelled 'gingerbrat' or 'gingerbret' which meant preserved ginger. But because of the confusion between 'bret' and 'bread', people started applying the word to cakes and cookies made with ginger as early as the 1400s.

GINGER

Ginger has been a valued spice for a long time, so it is not surprising that its name goes back all the way to Sanskrit. The Sanskrit name *śrngavera* was influenced by their word for 'horn', *śrnga*, because ginger root looks like an antler. By the time the thing and the word had travelled, via Latin *zingiber* and Old

French *gingimbre,* as far as medieval Britain, it had been simplified to 'gingifer' and then to 'ginger'.

'Gingerly', by the way, has nothing to do with ginger. At its origins in English, in the 1500s, 'gingerly' was probably an adverb used in dancing to mean 'daintily, delicately, with small, elegant steps'. It came from a French word *gensor,* which meant 'pretty or graceful', and was in turn derived from the Latin *gent,* which meant 'aristocratic' and has also given us 'genteel'. So there has always been this association between noble birth and refined manners and movement. Originally if you said someone danced 'gingerly', it was a compliment, but gradually it came to have derogatory overtones of mincing, until finally it came to apply to any motion that is timid, wary, or tentative.

MOLASSES

Molasses is a crucial ingredient in gingerbread. The Portuguese word for molasses is *melaço,* which comes from the Latin *mellaceus,* meaning roughly 'honey-like'. The English borrowed the Portuguese word in the 16th century, but they borrowed the plural form *melaços,* since molasses is actually the 'dregs' of raw sugar. In 1870, it was correct to say, 'The Americans are all fond of molasses; using them regularly at breakfast and supper to their buckwheat cakes and waffles.' But now 'molasses' is treated as a singular. This evolution in usage is similar to what is currently happening with 'data' and 'media', yet no one castigates anyone for using 'molasses' in the singular.

MINCEMEAT

Minçemeat pie is a traditional English Christmas food. Why is it called mincemeat, since it is a mixture of raisins and other dried fruits and spices? 'Mince' comes through French from Latin *minutia,* meaning smallness, or a small thing. In the 1700s, 'mincemeat' was 'minced meat'. It did have ground meat in it then; adding sugar, spices, and alcohol was a way of preserving the meat. This culinary custom was already several centuries old. In the Middle Ages, small pies filled with chopped meat, fish, or liver, mixed with fruit and spices, had been known by the delightful name 'chewettes', which I think we should revive. In the 1500s, by then known as 'shred pies', these sweet-savoury delicacies were already considered a Christmas must-have. Nowadays the only meat product left in mincemeat is usually suet, and there are even 'vegetarian' mincemeats, but, thank God, no mincetofu pies yet. It took a mere fifty years between the 16th and 17th centuries for 'minced meat' to become 'mincemeat', in an evolution that is paralleled today by the move from 'iced tea' to 'ice tea', which will probably end up as 'icetea'. We have evidence for the expression 'make mincemeat of someone' from the mid-1600s.

PUDDING

Nowadays we think of pudding especially as a sweet dish (except for Yorkshire pudding), but originally it was savoury. In fact the word first denoted a type of sausage. The name came from the Old French word *boudin,* which in turn probably came from the popular Latin *botellus* meaning 'sausage'. *Botellus* also meant 'small intestine' and is also the source of the word 'bowel'. Very appetizing, and perhaps not what you want to dwell upon when about to tuck into a Christmas pud! This very old sense of 'pudding' survives in the British English word for blood sausage, which they call 'black pudding'. So when in about 1300 the word 'pudding' cropped up in English, it meant, as the *OED* defines it, 'A dish made with the stomach or other part of the intestines of a pig, sheep, or other animal, stuffed with a mixture of minced meat, suet, oatmeal, seasoning, etc., and boiled.' Yum. But just as mincemeat started out as a savoury dish, and then gradually the meat was replaced by suet and then the suet by some other kind of fat until mincemeat had nothing of meat left in it and was a dessert rather than a savoury dish, something similar happened to pudding. Christmas pudding was in fact a substantial main course, containing meat, onions, and other root vegetables, as well as dried fruit, until the 19th century. Even today my family Christmas pudding recipe includes grated carrots and grated potatoes as well as suet.

You might be curious to know why Christmas pudding has also been called 'plum pudding' or 'figgy pudding' when there are usually no plums or figs in it. There were prunes originally, so the name 'plum pudding' was quite accurate, but in about the 16th century 'plum' came to mean a raisin or currant when these were substituted for prunes. 'Fig' was used in the dialect of southwest England to mean 'raisin', and this has survived in the Newfoundland dish 'figgy duff', since many of the original settlers of Newfoundland were from the West Country.

Bundle Up!

ॐ

The week between Christmas and New Year's is an opportunity to get out, celebrate winter, and think about some of our winter accoutrements and why we call them what we do.

TOQUE

Being Canadian, we have to start with the toque (or tuque). 'Toque', when it is used to mean what the British hilariously (to us, anyway) call a 'bobble hat', is a Canadianism, and it has a Canadian history. English Canadians borrowed from Canadian French the word *tuque*, which then got confused with another French word designating a kind of headgear, the *toque*. That tall white hat worn by chefs is a 'toque' (the word comes from an Italian name for a kind of silk fabric), but it wouldn't be much good at keeping your ears warm! Most dictionaries, not being Canadian, define the word 'toque' as a 'small brimless hat, made of velvet, and worn by women', and say it is pronounced 'toke' (woe betide the new Canadian shopping for one!). Some dictionaries even provide a helpful drawing of a Tudor lady wearing a cute hat with a feather sticking out of it. Pity the poor non-Canadian who tries to apply this definition when reading a Canadian novel that includes lines like 'they were dressed like loggers in toques and boots' or 'Our first Northern canoe trip...Wearing wetsuits and toques against the cold'. Visions of cross-dressing lumberjacks spring to mind. Our

'toque' ultimately derives from a very old pre-Roman word, *tukka*, designating a hill or gourd, which remained alive in some French dialects and was brought over to North America, where it became 'tuque' (as in the name of the town La Tuque in Quebec). It is doubtless because of the similarity of shape that the Canadian knitted cap was given this name.

TOBOGGAN

'Toboggan' also originated in Canada. It comes to us via Canadian French from an Algonquian language, probably Mi'kmaq or Abenaki. As early as the 1690s, the French in Canada were talking about the *tabaganne*, a very useful invention of the native

peoples for transporting things over snow. The Algonquian word is derived ultimately from two roots meaning 'a device' and 'pulling by a cord'. When English speakers moved north to Canada after the American Revolution, they too adopted both the word and the thing from the French Canadians. Canadians may find it amusing to know that, in some parts of the southern US, a toboggan is what we were just talking about, a toque, so you might come across a sentence like 'The burglar was wearing a red toboggan and tight pants'!

SKATE

'Skate' was borrowed in the late 1600s from the Dutch, who had been skating recreationally on their canals since the Middle Ages. The Dutch word *schaats* had been adapted from an Old French word *escache,* meaning 'stilt'. In Dutch, you had one *schaats* and two *schaatsen.* So in English, it should be one skates and two skateses. Of course, the English thought the *s* was the plural ending, so they used 'skates' for the pair, and lopped off the *s* to form the singular 'skate'.

MITTEN

'Mitten' came into English in the late 1200s from the French word *mitaine.* There are two theories as to where the French got this word. One is that it came from Provençal *mitana,* which was a skin-lined glove cut off at the middle, and that the word was derived from the Latin *medietas* meaning 'half' (because it was cut in half). A more likely explanation, unfortunately for cat lovers like me, is that *mitaine* came from the Old French word *mite,* a pet name for a cat, like our 'puss' or 'kitty'. This word was probably of Germanic origin, in imitation of a cat mewing. Even today in German, when you're calling your cat to come to you (if it should deign to do so), you say, '*Miez, Miez, Miez!*' (pronounced MEETS). Mittens were originally lined with fur, very possibly cat fur.

IDIOT STRINGS

In Canada, it's a really undesirable thing to lose one or both of your mitts in the depths of winter, so many children have mitts attached to a string that runs through the sleeves of their coat. In the charitable way of children, these have come to be called 'idiot strings' in Canada. The idea (though not of course the English word) seems to have been invented by the Inuit, because losing a mitt out on the frozen tundra really would be a problem.

SCARF

In the Middle Ages, pilgrims used to carry a kind of purse in which they would keep the alms that they begged along the way to the shrine they were visiting. This was slung diagonally across their chest and called an *escarpe* in medieval Northern French. When the word came into English as 'scarf' in the 1500s, it was used for the kind of sash worn diagonally across the chest by military officers. Today you see those only in dress uniforms, but in the 1500s it was actually used for carrying things, much like the pilgrim's purse. At about the same time, 'scarf' was also used to mean a purely decorative shawl-like garment of a light fabric like silk or gauze.

Surprisingly, it wasn't until the 1800s that 'scarf' came to apply to the warm band of cloth that keeps our necks and noses warm in the winter. Although the article of clothing existed before then, it had been called a 'muffler' since the end of the 16th century. 'Muffler' is now a very old-fashioned name for a scarf, possibly because of the confusion with the car sense of 'muffler', which cropped up in the 1890s.

GALOSHES

The Romans had a word *gallica solea,* which meant 'Gallic shoe'. This probably meant a clog or large wooden kind of platform sole that people attached to their shoes so that they could navigate through mud and water. Presumably it was called 'Gallic' because mud and water were more of a problem for pedestrians in Gaul than in dry, sunny Italy, and so this may have been a Gaulish invention. Anyway, *gallica solea* got shortened to *gallica* and then became *gallicula*. By the time Latin had become Old French, the word had been corrupted into *galoche*. The English borrowed it from the French in the 1300s, and it continued to mean these wooden pattens that kept your feet dry in bad weather until the 19th century. Then, with rubber becoming widespread as a result of British colonization of India and the Far East, a new kind of rubber footwear, performing the same function but with a different design, took on the name 'galoshes'.

RUBBER

Many a gentleman's fine shoes would be ruined in the winter without rubbers (or 'toe rubbers', to use a Canadianism). The substance we know as rubber was called 'caoutchouc' in English when it first burst upon the scene in the 1700s. We got it from the French, who to this day call rubber *caoutchouc*. They had got the name from an aboriginal tribe of Ecuador when two French scientists visited South America in 1735 and sent a sample, with an account of the tree from which it came, back to France from Quito. So we could have been lumbered with 'caoutchouc', which would have been a nightmare to spell. Fortunately the English of the 1700s discovered that one of the best uses for the substance was rubbing out pencil marks, so they called it simply 'rubber', or 'India rubber' when it started being shipped from the East Indies. Some say that it was actually the chemist Joseph Priestley who christened caoutchouc 'rubber', but since he was the guy who called oxygen 'dephlogisticated air' when he discovered it, it seems unlikely that he would have opted for something as simple as 'rubber'!

Through the late 1700s and early 1800s there were a couple of other words vying to be the name for rubber. One was 'plastic gum' ('plastic' in its original sense of 'that can be shaped or moulded').

The other was 'gum elastic'. Both of these names alluded to the fact that the substance came from the rubber tree's gum. This is why you still find in some areas—in Canada typically on the West Coast—that rubber boots are called 'gumboots'. And because rubber-soled shoes or 'gum shoes' allow people to get around without making any noise, and sneak up on people, they came to be called 'sneakers', and 'gumshoe' came to designate police detective work.

WINDROW
'Windrows', at least in Canada, are those huge piles of snow left by the passage of a snowplough—the ones they leave across the foot of your driveway or walk just after you've shovelled it. Readers may have other less polite names for them, but why are they called a 'windrow' instead of a 'ploughrow', then? This is a particularly Canadian use of the word, which in other varieties of the language means a row of mown hay or grass left to be dried by the wind.

HOARFROST
Hoar in Old English meant 'old'. This sense still survives in a 'hoary old joke'. From meaning 'old', *hoar* came to mean 'grey-haired from age' and then came to mean simply 'greyish-white'. The frost that forms on trees looked to the Anglo-Saxons like white hair on the head, so they called it 'hoarfrost'. (See also HOREHOUND in THE DOG DAYS OF SUMMER, page 66.)

HAPPY NEW YEAR!

ॐ

Traditionally the biggest boozefest of the year is the New Year's Eve party, though people are knocking back alcohol in large quantities throughout the festive season. So, if you're not too bleary-eyed, let's look at some words for alcohol, types of drinks, and finally some words that started out with a connection to alcohol that they have since lost.

ALCOHOL

In Arabic *al-koh'l* (derived from a Hebrew word, *kakhal*, meaning to stain or paint) meant 'the kohl', the fine metallic powder used as eyeshadow in the East. When 'alcohol' entered English in the 1600s, it meant 'kohl'. But it soon came to be used to mean any pulverized substance, and then to mean an essence obtained by distillation. By the 17th century people talked of the 'alcohol of wine', that is, the spirit obtained by distillation of wine. By the 18th century people talked of 'alcohol' by itself, meaning the intoxicating substance in fermented drinks. There had been a name for this before: in the 1400s, it had been known as 'burning water' or 'ardent water', or by the Latin phrase meaning 'water of life': 'aqua-vitae'. The designation 'water of life' is also at the origin of the word 'whisky', which comes from the Gaelic *uisge* meaning 'water', and '*beatha*' meaning 'life'.

BOOZE

'Booze' came into English as a verb in the 1300s, probably from Middle Dutch *busen*, meaning 'drink to excess'. The word was not very common in the Middle Ages, but by Shakespeare's time it was well known as thieves' and beggars' cant, and then became more general slang. Here's a great example from 1592: 'They lie boozing and beer-bathing in their houses every afternoon.' It wasn't until the 1750s that 'booze' started to be used as a noun. The word was originally spelled 'bouse' but pronounced BOOZE, because that was the way 'bouse' was pronounced before the Great Vowel Shift. For some reason, this word was not affected by the Great Vowel Shift, so the spelling changed to reflect the pronunciation in about the 18th century.

MOONSHINE

'Moonshine' acquired the meaning of 'smuggled liquor' in the mid-1700s, since smuggling was usually done by moonlight. From there it was an easy step to the sense of 'illicitly produced liquor'.

BOOTLEG

'Bootleg' started to be used to mean illicit alcohol in the United States in the 1890s, from the habit its purveyors had of concealing the bottles in their boot legs.

HOOCH

Someone inquired of me whether it was true that 'hooch' was derived from the chemical name for alcohol. This is yet another example of the dreaded folk etymology, which lurks everywhere and must be rooted out! It's utterly ridiculous for a number of reasons: ethanol is $C_2H_5OH_5$—try making 'hooch' out of that! And in any case, no one has ever said, 'I feel like a shot of CHOH!'

The truth is a lot more interesting. There was a Tlingit word, roughly *Hutsnuwu*, meaning 'grizzly bear fort', which was borrowed into English as 'Hoochinoo' to designate a Native people living on Admiralty Island, Alaska, who were reputed to produce strong drink. 'Hoochinoo' came to be applied to this alcoholic liquor, described by one Alaskan public servant in 1879 as 'the most infernal decoction ever invented, producing intoxication, debauchery, insanity, and death'. By the 1890s it was shortened to 'hooch' and used of any rotgut liquor. The Klondike gold rush, which happened about the same time, helped to popularize the word and make it part of the general English language, thanks in no small part to the popularity of writers like Jack London and Robert Service. Our first quotation, from an 1897 book called *Pioneers of the Klondyke*, is the no doubt indisputable 'The manufacture of "hooch", which is undertaken by the saloon-keepers themselves, is weirdly horrible.'

BEER

'Beer' is a Germanic word derived from a monastic Latin word, *biber*, meaning 'to drink'. Although it had come into English by the time of the Anglo-Saxons (who probably brought it with them from the continent), its use was quite rare until about the 1500s, because 'ale' (beer without hops) was the more common drink. One place where the word 'beer' did turn up was in poetry. Imagine 'beer' being a poetic word! When it started being drunk more commonly in England, beer didn't get great press, witness this 1542 quote: 'Beer is made of malt, and hops, and water: it is a natural drink for a Dutch man. And now of late days it is much used in England to the detriment of many English men.'

LAGER

'Lager' comes from the German word *lager* meaning 'to store', because it is stored for several months to mature before drinking.

SUDS

In medieval Dutch and German, a *sudse* was a marsh or bog. East Anglia, a part of England covered by marshes until it was drained in the 17th century (by a Dutch engineer, as it happens), had long had strong ties with Holland. People living there borrowed *sudse* in the 1500s to mean 'fen waters mixed with mud' (of course, the English thought the s at the end signified a plural). In the rest of the country it came to mean the dregs, or filth, or muck. Shortly afterwards, it came to apply to soap suds, with the emphasis on the dirt that clung to the suds, the suds being seen as the 'dregs' of washing. By then, it was also being used to designate foam or froth. In 1609 the froth on ale was being likened to suds, but it was not until the early 20th century that 'suds' came to be a slang term for beer.

GROG

'Grog' is an abbreviation of the word *grogram*, which is a type of stiff, coarse fabric the name of which is derived from the French *gros grain* meaning 'coarse grain'. But why on earth would a drink be named after a fabric? The story goes that there was a British admiral, Edward Vernon, in the 1700s, who always wore a cloak of this fabric, so the sailors gave him the nickname 'Old Grog'. It was the tradition in the Royal Navy to serve out a tot of rum to the sailors every day. But in 1740, Admiral Vernon ordered that the rum should be diluted with water. This didn't go over too well with the sailors, and they christened the mixture after the admiral, calling it 'grog'. Soon after that the word 'groggy' was born, meaning 'drunk', but it has of course now lost this sense, to mean only 'dazed, not alert', as if under the influence of alcohol.

CIDER

'Cider' comes from the Hebrew *shekar*, meaning 'intoxicating liquor, strong drink'. This word was used in the Bible, but the Greek and Latin translators hadn't a clue how to translate it, so they simply borrowed it as *sicera*. In Old French this became *sidre*, and it applied to any strong drink. But by the time it was adopted into non-ecclesiastical English from French in the 1300s, it meant specifically 'alcoholic drink made from fermented apples'. It was, after all, the Norman French, renowned to this day for their cider production, who invaded England, and Normandy was part of England till the late 1200s. Eventually, the idea of 'apple drink' became stronger than 'alcoholic drink' so that, in North America, 'cider' can also be applied to plain old apple juice.

TOAST

Not the stuff you eat for breakfast, but in the drinking sense. But they're connected. 'Toast' started out in English in the 1300s as a verb meaning to burn or parch with the heat of the sun, sort of like 'tan' today. We acquired it from the Old French *toster,* which meant 'roast', derived from a past participle of the Latin *torrere,* meaning to dry with heat, which has also given us 'torrid', 'torrefaction'—and even 'torrent', oddly enough, but that's another story. The 'grilled bread' sense of 'toast' cropped up in the 1400s, but at the time, toast wasn't something you ate for breakfast. It was a piece of bread coated with sugar and spices (much like cinnamon toast nowadays, but one recipe lists pepper, saffron, and salt) and then grilled and dropped in a glass of wine to flavour it. This custom explains why we 'drink a toast'. In about 1700, it became fashionable to mention a lady's name when inviting people to drink; usually the lady was the reigning belle of the social season. The idea was that thinking of the lady while drinking added a special savour to the wine just as the spiced pieces of toast did. Originally 'toast' meant the actual person in whose honour the drink was taken, then by the mid-1800s it came to mean the drink itself.

The expression 'you're toast' is much more recent. There's been a British expression 'have someone on toast', meaning to have them in a vulnerable position, since about 1880. But it would seem that 'you're toast' comes to us from the movie *Ghostbusters*. The *Oxford English Dictionary* lexicographers (who most people probably wouldn't think spend time investigating *Ghostbusters*) have looked into this and discovered that, in the script written by Dan Aykroyd and Harold Ramis in 1983, there is a line: 'That's it! I'm gonna turn this guy into toast!' Now, in the movie itself, made in 1984, there was much ad-libbing, and Bill Murray turned the line into 'This chick is toast.' And it seems to have caught on from there.

CHEERS

'Cheer' has its origin in an ancient Greek word for 'head', *kara*. This came into Latin and then into French, where it was transformed into *chere* and meant the face. And 'face' is what *chere* meant when it came into English just after the Norman Conquest.

At about the same time, it also meant the expression on the face, so you could have sentences that we would find confusing, such as 'His chere was so sad and sori', meaning 'his face was sad and sorry'. From there it came to mean one's emotional state, either good or bad, so we have both 'be of good cheer' and 'She was in a dreary cheer'. But gradually the association with gladness and encouragement began to predominate until, by the 1500s, 'cheer' could mean something that made you happy, especially food. And by the 1700s a cheer was a shout of encouragement or approval. But it isn't until 1919 that we find evidence of 'cheers' as a drinking toast. A recent development, since about the 1970s, is the use of 'cheers' in British English as an all-purpose salutation meaning good-bye, thank you, and so on. This has now spread across the Atlantic, at least in emails.

CAROUSE
'Carouse' cropped up in the 1500s, when we borrowed it from German via French. The Germans had a phrase *gar aus trinken,* which meant roughly 'drink all out'. *Aus* means 'out', and *gar* is an intensifier, meaning something like 'really'. Originally in English 'carouse' was an adverb in the phrase 'to drink carouse', meaning to down a drink in one go, to chugalug it. Our first quotation for it, from 1567, is the entertaining 'The tippling sots at midnight to quaff carouse do use.' (Some things haven't changed in 500 years.) But shortly after that, the shortened form 'to carouse' sprang up, eventually coming to mean not specifically drinking a whole bowlful of something but just drinking plentiful amounts of alcohol while enjoying oneself in a lively way.

LAMPOON
'Lampoon' comes from the French word *lampons,* meaning 'let us drink' or more precisely 'let us booze'! The verb *lamper* was a variant of *laper,* meaning 'to lap', which probably had its origins in the

sounds made by, say, a cat lapping water. In 16th-century France, it was very common for satirical songs to have '*Lampons!*' or 'Let us drink!' as a refrain. Or perhaps drinking songs took on a satirical bent. Whichever way it happened, a verb *lamponner* soon arose to mean 'ridicule', and this gave us the English word 'lampoon' from the mid-1600s on.

SYMPOSIUM

'Symposium' has its roots in Greek. This will be no surprise to people who are familiar with Plato's *Symposium*. The word literally means 'a drinking party', coming from the Greek word *sum* meaning 'together' and *potes* meaning 'drinker'. Now, *symposia* were a cultural institution in Greece, and they did indeed involve a lot of drinking (judging from the academic conferences I have attended, this tradition is still alive and well), but they also had redeeming ritual, philosophic, literary, intellectual, and aesthetic virtues. At least that's what classical scholars tell us; a cynic could see them as just an excuse to get drunk. So if you're a little under the weather from partying a bit too much the night before, you could always say you've been at a symposium!

HOBNOB

Hobnob also has its origins in drinking, in the mid-18th century. It started out as 'hab nab', which meant 'have it or not', sort of like 'willy-nilly'. 'Hob nob' was a variant of 'hab nab', used of people drinking to each other alternately. So one drinker would take a swig, he'd be the hab part, while the other waited, being the nab part. And then it was turn and turn about. Soon, instead of saying that you would 'drink hob nob' with someone, people just said that they would 'hob and nob' or 'hobnob' with someone, meaning go out drinking with them. Gradually 'hobnob' came to mean just associating with someone socially, especially with someone of higher social standing.

New Year's Babies

Much fuss is made over the first baby born in the new year, so January 1 is a good time to look at words relating to the little bundles of joy.

BABY

There were no babies in England before 1377! It seems that 'baby' and the related word 'babe' cropped up in the 1300s, possibly as a diminutive of an earlier word *baban*. *Baban* probably arose as an imitation of a baby babbling, a word which appeared at the same time. Of course they did have a word for newborns before this: in Old English, 'child' meant specifically the unborn or newborn baby. This meaning survives now only in references to the 'Christ child' in the manger, for gradually the word came to apply to older children. This evolution probably accounts for why 'baby' cropped up to fill the gap.

INFANT, INFANTRY

'Infant' appeared in English at about the same time as 'baby', and technically designates a baby before it can speak. It comes ultimately from a Latin word *infans*, meaning 'unable to speak'. But even before Latin broke up into all the Romance languages, *infans* had come to mean a child of any age, which is why the French *enfant* means 'child' rather than 'infant' specifically.

But why are foot soldiers known as 'infantry'? In the Middle Ages, a young soldier who was not yet a knight, and therefore fought on foot, was also called an *enfant*, or in Italian, an *infante*. Foot soldiers collectively came to be known as *infanteria* and hence, in English, 'infantry'.

DIAPER

The word 'diaper' comes ultimately from two Greek words, *dia* meaning 'through' and *aspros* meaning 'white'. So literally it means 'white through and through' (which diapers, it must be said, often aren't). In Old French and medieval Latin, 'diaper' was a costly silk fabric with gold thread woven into it—definitely not the sort of thing to put on a baby's bottom! In medieval English, however, 'diaper' was a type of fabric, especially linen or cotton, woven in such a way as to create a diamond pattern. Perhaps the way the fabric was woven gave it superior absorbent qualities. We have a quotation from Shakespeare talking about 'a diaper' being a towel to dry one's fingers on. Then in the mid-1800s we start seeing

American references to babies' diapers. This, I suspect, is a case where the American colonists brought over a word that was common in Shakespeare's time (which coincided with the first colonization of America) and hung onto it while it died out in England, to be replaced there by 'nappy', a short form of 'napkin'.

PAMPER

The word 'Pampers' has been registered as a trademark for diapers since 1963, but the verb 'pamper' has been around for centuries. It came into English in the late Middle Ages, probably from Germany or Holland. It was likely derived from the word *pamp,* meaning 'eat greedily' in many Germanic languages, which may be related to the Latin word *pappare,* meaning 'to feed with pap', which in turn is derived from baby talk *papa* for 'food' (even babies spoke Latin in ancient Rome). When 'pamper' first appeared, it meant to cram or gorge someone with food. Subsequently it came to mean 'indulging' generally, but it seems that it is only in the 20th century that it lost the somewhat pejorative connotations of a moral-fibre-sapping indulgence. And then all of a sudden in the 20th century (what does this say about the 20th century?), 'pamper' has come to have very positive connotations

CRY

In ancient Rome, the word for the citizens was *Quirites*. From this arose a verb, *quiritare*, which meant literally 'call on the Quirites for help', or just raise a public outcry generally, calling on the Roman citizens to help you out. Even in Latin, the word also had the meaning of wailing and lamenting. The Gauls got hold of *quiritare* and, as usual, scrunched it down and dropped a few consonants until it ended up as *crier* in French, and this is what we borrowed from them shortly after the Norman Conquest. We already had two perfectly good Old English words for the phenomenon, 'weep' and 'yell', and the Old Norse speakers in the north of Britain had 'wail', but English has never hesitated to adopt three synonyms where one word might do! Anyway, when the baby's crying because he or she needs a diaper changed, you could always try just waiting to see if the Quirites turn up to do the job!

SOOTHE

'Soothe' has come a very long way from its origins in Old English. It started out as *sooth*, meaning 'truth', which survives today only in 'soothsayer' (originally 'a person who speaks the truth about the future') and in the jocular 'forsooth'. So 'soothe' originally meant 'prove or declare to be true'. Then, in the 1500s, it came to mean expressing assent with someone, especially to flatter them. So, if someone said something ridiculous and you said, 'Yes, that's true,' you were soothing them. As a result, 'soothe' soon came to mean humouring or appeasing someone, especially by smoothing or glossing over their offences. This is how we ended up with 'soothe' meaning 'calm someone down' and subsequently, by the 1700s, 'calm down an irritation or pain'. The word 'soother' started being used of a baby's pacifier in the 19th century, possibly because the prudish Victorians became squeamish about using the words 'nipple' or 'teat' (not to mention the latter's dialectal variant 'tit').

CHINESE NEW YEAR

ဆ

Chinese or Lunar New Year falls in either late January or early February. A time to look at some of the Chinese words that have enriched the English language.

TEA

The Mandarin word for tea is *ch'a*, and this was the form that first appeared in English in the 1500s, in accounts of people's travels to the Orient. Even today in Cockney slang, 'cha' is a word for tea. Meanwhile, however, the Dutch were also active in the East Indies, and they encountered the substance under a different name in another dialect of Chinese, possibly in Taiwan. This word was *te*. To this day in fact, in Taiwanese, the word for tea is *de*. The Dutch were the first to import tea to Europe, in the early 1600s, and they initially cornered the market. They turned the Chinese word into *tee* (pronounced TAY), and this caught on throughout continental Europe. For instance, tea was all the rage in Paris in the 1630s; the French took the Dutch word and made it *thé*. At the time, England was the world's biggest consumer of coffee, so the English were latecomers to the 17th-century tea trend; tea was first publicly sold in England only in 1657. Since the English latched on to the drink (with a vengeance, one might say) only after it had been adopted throughout the continent, with the Dutch name, the word we use now is the form that came through Dutch rather than the Mandarin word. 'Tea' was originally pronounced TAY in English as well (and indeed still is in some dialects of English) but by the end of the 1700s the pronunciation TEE had won out.

(ORANGE) PEKOE

The most common type of tea, orange pekoe gets its name from two Chinese words, from the Amoy dialect spoken in the province of China directly across the Formosa Strait from Taiwan. *Pek* meant 'white' and *ho* meant 'down'; this variety of tea was so called because originally it was made of tea leaves picked so young that they still had that white downy fuzz found on young leaves.

The 'orange' in 'orange pekoe' had nothing to do with Chinese, however. It has not been determined for sure where it comes from; it may designate the colour of the leaf buds or the drink, or it may be because, at the beginning of the tea trade, the Dutch cornered the market and they named it 'Orange' in honour of the House of Orange, which was the Dutch royal house.

KETCHUP

This apparently comes from a Chinese dialect word *k'e-chap*, which means 'brine of pickled fish'. Probably disgusting on french fries. The word may have migrated into English from Chinese via Malay thanks, like 'tea', to the Dutch. The condiment was discovered by the English surprisingly early: our first quotation, which is for the form 'catchup', is from 1690. At this point, and for some 150 years afterward, no tomatoes were involved, for they were expensive and besides were viewed as a suspicious American import by the English till the late 19th century. Originally, mushrooms or walnuts were the characteristic ingredient of ketchup, sometimes with anchovies and oysters. 'Ketchup' to Jonathan Swift, Lord Byron, and Charles Dickens (among the many great names in English literature who have felt the need to mention it) was probably something like Worcestershire sauce. But in the late 19th century, tomatoes started to be produced in large quantities in the United States. Instead of being an expensive rarity, they became a cheap, abundant, and notoriously perishable commodity. Preserving them in a sweetish puréed pickle (which tomato ketchup essentially is) was a good way to sell them, as Heinz did starting in 1876. And so it was that 'ketchup' came to be a tomato sauce.

CHOPSTICK

When the English started trading with the Chinese in the 1600s, a pidgin language grew up. (A pidgin is a mixture of two languages to facilitate communication between two cultures in contact for trade.) In Chinese pidgin, *chop* meant 'quick'. 'Chopstick' was, therefore, a translation of the Chinese name for chopsticks, *kwaizi*, which literally meant 'nimble children' or 'nimble ones'.

KOWTOW

'Kowtow' comes from two Chinese words, *k'o* meaning 'knock' and *t'ou* meaning 'head'. *K'o-t'ou* designated the Chinese custom of touching the ground with one's forehead when prostrating oneself in respect or worship. The word first appeared in English in this sense in 1804, in a book recounting someone's travels in China. The first use we have of it in the figurative sense of acting obsequiously or submitting to another's will is in an 1826 novel by Benjamin Disraeli, who took the noun and—gasp—made it a verb.

Auld Lang Syne

ॐ

January 25th is Robbie Burns Day, a time for celebrating all things Scottish, including some of the many words that started out in Scots English. We also look at a word that seems to be related to the Scots but in fact is not.

DINKY

'Dink' was a Scottish adjective, dating from the 1500s, meaning 'finely dressed'. It was almost always applied to women, especially in the phrase 'dink and dainty'. So 'dinky' arose in the late 18th century to mean 'well dressed in a dainty sort of way'. Soon the notion of clothing was lost and all that was left was the notion of daintiness or smallness. In turn, the notion of daintiness was lost, leaving only the notion of smallness, with connotations of insignificance and triviality.

GRUESOME

There is a Scottish verb, *grue*, which means to shudder or tremble with fear. So 'gruesome', when it arose originally in Scottish English in the 1500s, meant literally 'so horrible as to make one shudder'. It would have remained strictly a Scottish word, but it was popularized by Sir Walter Scott in the early 19th century.

SKULDUGGERY

Originally, 'skulduggery' was a Scottish word, 'sculduddery', which meant unchaste behaviour or, as the Scottish sources explain it, 'fornication and adultery'. When the word came to North America in the 1860s, it became 'skulduggery' and lost its sexual connotations to mean merely underhanded doings, especially in politics.

SKIFF

'Skiff', meaning a light flurry or dusting of snow, is found in Canada in areas of Scottish settlement such as the Prairies and the Maritimes. It is a Scottish word, unrelated to the type of boat called a 'skiff'. The noun was derived from a verb 'skiff', meaning to move lightly and quickly (presumably because a light dusting of snow can be picked up and moved around by the wind). This in turn came from a word 'skift', which was a variant of the word 'shift'. In the Middle Ages, there was a divide between the English spoken by the people in Scotland and the north of England, which was heavily influenced by the Vikings, and the people in the South, whose Anglo-Saxon had much less Scandinavian influence. The Vikings could say 'sk' at the beginning of a word, but the Anglo-Saxons could only say 'sh'. This led to pairs of words meaning the same thing in modern English, like 'scream' (from Norse) and 'shriek' (from Anglo-Saxon). This is why there was a Scottish variant 'skift' for the southern-English 'shift'.

FECKLESS

Feck was a Scottish word, apparently a shortening of 'effect', which meant 'efficiency' or 'effectiveness', and thus vigour in getting things done. In Scottish English, you could be feckful—that is, efficient or powerful—or feckless. For some reason 'feckless' is the only one of these forms to have established itself outside Scottish English.

SLOGAN

'Slogan' comes from two Gaelic words, *sluagh* meaning 'army' and *ghairm* meaning 'shout'. It originally meant a battle cry, usually one consisting of the name of the person to whom the soldiers rallied. So you and your fellow marauders might charge down the highland slopes yelling 'MACDONALD!' or whatever your clan name was. By the mid-1800s it was being used to mean a catchy word or phrase used by politicians and marketers.

SCOT-FREE

This has nothing to do with the inhabitants of Scotland. In Northern Middle English, a 'scot' was a payment for food or entertainment, or a contribution towards its cost. This is related to our word 'shot' (in the same way that 'skiff' and 'shift' are related), because one of the Old English meanings of 'shoot' was 'pay' or 'contribute a portion'. This is why we still talk about 'paying the whole shot' (had you ever wondered what that had to do with shooting?), and why we have 'shots' of alcohol. A 'scot' was also a kind of municipal tax. So originally someone who was scot-free was someone who got out of paying his bar tab or his local taxes. From about the 1600s it started to mean 'free from injury or punishment'. (See also HOPSCOTCH in GAMES CHILDREN PLAY, page 102).

PLACE YOUR BETS

ॐ

The Super Bowl rolls around every year about the beginning of February and, it is said, gambling reaches its peak.

GAMBLE

Oddly, 'gamble' seems to have cropped up almost out of nowhere in the 1700s, at which time it was a highly pejorative word. It was probably a dialect variant of the word which has also given us 'game', *gamen*, which was simply the Old English word for fun or amusement.

BET

Again, a bit of a mystery word, which cropped up at about Shakespeare's time. The most persuasive theory is that it is a shortened form of 'abet', in the sense, I guess, that if a wager of money were involved, this would spur on the participants. 'Abet' didn't originally have the pejorative sense that it has now as in 'aid and abet' in the criminal world. It just meant 'to spur on'. It came from an Old French word, *abeter*, which meant literally to bait the hounds so that they would be more eager in the hunt.

POOL

You would think probably that the kind of pool that you engage in at the office is ultimately the same pool that you go swimming in, because you think, 'well, it's the idea that it's a great big container that stuff is put in'. In fact, the two are completely different words.

The pool of water was originally the Old English word *pol*, which meant precisely what it means today. The gambling pool, on the other hand, didn't appear in English till the late 1600s. English borrowed it from the French word *poule*, meaning 'chicken'. In French, one of the slang meanings of the word *poule* was 'booty' or 'plunder': you have images of soldiers carting off chickens after they have sacked the village. And this came to mean the collective stakes to be won in a card game—what the winner carried off like the victor's spoils of war. From there it developed into all kinds of collective groupings: for gambling, as in office pools, or not for gambling, as in car pools—although sometimes those might be a gamble, depending on the drivers involved!

But I should advise you not to use 'pool' in the gambling sense when talking to an Australian. I was in Australia once when their biggest horse race was on, and I asked an Australian, 'Do you have a pool at the office?' She looked a little puzzled, and then said, 'We used to, but then they paved it over and made it into a parking lot!' In Australia they have office 'sweeps' instead.

KITTY

The 'kitty' into which a group of people contribute money has nothing to do with pussycats! Its origin is a bit obscure, but it is probably a diminutive of the word 'kit', which—before it came to mean a soldier's accoutrements or someone's tools, or parts to be assembled—meant a kind of tub for washing dishes or transporting food. So, just as we use the word 'pot' to mean a collective pool, it made sense to talk about a 'kitty'.

SUPER

Since we are talking about the Super Bowl, what about the word 'super'? It arose as a shortening of the word 'superfine', which meant literally 'above fine', *super* being the Latin word for 'above'. 'Superfine' was a trendy word in commercial circles from the 1600s to the 1800s. Just about everyone wanted to advertise their goods as being 'superfine', much as nowadays in Britain everyone describes their products as 'superb'. The shortened form 'super' probably cropped up as commercial slang, then caught on. But the Super Bowl, as being the bowl with extraordinary characteristics greater than any other bowl, probably owes more to the word 'superman', which was originally used to translate Nietzsche's idea of the '*Übermensch*', an ideal superior man. George Bernard Shaw's play *Man and Superman* in 1903 seems to mark the first use of the word 'superman' in English.

FLU SEASON

&

February is often the peak of the flu season. If you're not too busy feeling like death warmed up, you might want to consider some of the words designating our illnesses, their symptoms, and some remedies and preventative measures.

FLU

'Flu' arose in the early 19th century as a shortening of 'influenza', which came into English from Italian in 1743. *Influenza*, like its English cognate 'influence', comes from the Latin word *influere*, meaning 'flow in'. Medieval astrologers believed that an ethereal fluid flowed out from the stars or heavens to affect people's characters and events generally, so, throughout the Middle Ages, *influenza* (and 'influence') had the meaning of an astrological influence. Since diseases were seen as being determined by this kind of influence, *influenza* (in phrases like *influenza di catarro*) took on the meaning of a 'visitation' of an epidemic disease. In 1743 a particularly nasty outbreak of flu happened in Italy, and people just called it *la influenza*. As flu does, it spread all over Europe, and the English adopted the Italian name.

VIRUS

In Latin, *virus* means 'a slimy liquid', 'poison', or 'an offensive odour or taste'. When the word was adopted into English around 1600, it designated a snake's venom. By the 18th century, it was used to mean a poisonous substance thought to be produced in the body as the result of a disease. As the 19th century saw advances in microbiology (it was Louis Pasteur who first used 'virus' in the modern sense), the word came to have its current meaning of a submicroscopic organism that makes us sick. And in the mid-20th century we started to use it to mean the sickness itself, as in, 'I've got a virus.' Computers, you may be surprised to learn, have been suffering from 'viruses' since 1972.

SHINGLES

Shingles (not the kind on your roof) are caused by the chicken pox virus. The ailment is characteristically accompanied by a rash around the middle of the body, and this is what gives the affliction its name, for 'shingles' is a corruption of the medieval Latin *cingulus*, which meant 'belt' or 'girdle'. The word for the roofing tiles come from the Latin *scindula*, which simply meant a wooden roofing tile.

SYNDROME

Some viruses, such as SARS, cause an assortment of symptoms, called a 'syndrome'. This word comes from the Greek *syn* meaning 'together' and *dromos* meaning 'running'; a syndrome is a series of symptoms that 'run together'. Syndrome was pronounced SIN-drummy in English when it was first borrowed in the 1500s. The element *dromos* also appears with the Greek word for 'horse', *hippo*, in the word 'hippodrome' for a racetrack.

SNEEZE

The original word in Old English was *fnese* (pronounced FNAYZ). I would love to revive this, because it sounds so much like the thing it describes, and that is probably how the word was created in the first place. *Fnese* survived through the Middle Ages, so that people in Chaucer's works were still fnesing. However, the combination *fn-* was becoming very odd. *Sn-*, on the other hand, was a fairly common combination, especially in nose-related words like 'snivel', 'sniff', 'snort', and 'snot' (there was an Old English verb *snite*, meaning 'blow one's nose', from which 'snot' seems to derive). Meanwhile there was also competition in Northern England and Scotland from 'neeze', which came from Old Norse. By the early 15th century, people weren't saying 'fnese' anymore. In some manuscripts and printing, 'fnese' was mistakenly printed as 'fnese', with the initial letter being the *f*-like form of *s* used at the beginning of words back then. People may also have mis-heard 'fnese' as 'sneeze', so by about 1500 'sneeze' started to appear, and by the 17th century it was the standard term.

NAUSEA

'Nausea' literally means 'seasickness', because it is ultimately from the Greek word for a ship, *naus*, which has also given us 'nautical'. All the same, 'nausea' entered the language in the mid-1500s meaning what it means today: 'loathing of food and inclination to vomit' as the OED delicately puts it!

'Vomit', which was rivalled for a while by 'evomit', is a 15th-century Anglo-French borrowing (ultimately from Latin), which took over from, but did not completely banish, the Anglo-Saxon 'spew'.

FAINT

'Faint' was originally a past tense of the verb 'to feign', which comes from Old French and ultimately from a Latin word meaning 'to form or mould', *fingere*, which has also given us 'figment' and 'fiction'. 'Faint' was therefore originally an adjective meaning 'feigned'. For instance, 'a faint friend' was a false friend. 'Feign' was also used to mean 'avoid one's duty by false pretences', so a shirker or malingerer would be called 'faint'. Such behaviour could be interpreted as laziness or cowardice, and thus we have expressions such as 'faint heart never won fair lady'. It could also be attributed (especially by the malingerer) to weakness or feebleness, so these senses, quickly followed by 'tending to lose consciousness', also became attached to 'faint'.

The verb 'faint' went through the same evolution, originally meaning 'to lose courage' but by 1400 meaning 'to lose consciousness'. Naturally, the English did pass out before 1400, but they used the Anglo-Saxon word 'swoon'. Yet another instance of borrowing a French synonym for an already existing English word, which was then restricted to a specialized usage.

LOZENGE

A lozenge was originally a diamond-shaped figure in heraldry. Heraldry was a preoccupation of the French-speaking aristocracy rather than the Anglo-Saxon peasants, so this is yet another word we got from the French in the Middle Ages. There are two theories as to where the French got it: perhaps from a word that meant 'slab' or, more ominously, considering what 'lozenge' means today, 'tombstone'. A second possibility is that it goes ultimately back to a word in Pahlavi (a Persian language), *lawz,* which meant 'almond', because the shape of an almond is similar to a diamond. The reason we now use the word for a type of cough drop is that in the 1500s medicated pills were made in a diamond shape. Eventually, the idea of the medication became more important than the shape of the thing.

POULTICE

A popular treatment for colds formerly was the mustard plaster, a kind of poultice. 'Poultice' is related to the word 'pulse', not as in the beating of the blood in the veins but 'pulse' as a synonym for leguminous plants like beans and lentils. *Puls* was the Latin word for a porridge made from these kinds of beans. The plural for this, *pultes,* came straight into English from Latin in the 1500s to designate a mixture with the consistency of mushy porridge or lentil stew, spread on a cloth for medical applications. No one really knows why *pultice* changed to 'poultice', but that is what won out by about 1750 and that is what we are stuck with.

IMMUNE

'Immune' comes from the Latin *munis,* meaning 'ready to be of service', which in turn comes from a noun *munus*, meaning 'sense of duty'. These words also survive in our word 'municipal'. In ancient Rome, if you were *immunis* (or 'not *munis'*) you were *exempt* from some service, duty or liability, and this is what the words 'immune' and 'immunity' conveyed when they were first borrowed into English around 1400. This use survives today in 'diplomatic immunity'. A figurative extension of this started to appear in the 1600s, with people talking about immunity from evil, distressing circumstances, and so on. In the mid-1800s we find Charlotte Brontë saying, 'It is a long time since I have known such immunity from headaches.' So the idea of somehow being protected or exempt from bad things had attached itself to this word, but it wasn't used very commonly. It was just lying there latently in the language waiting for a good role to come along. In the mid- to late-1800s, it got its big chance, thanks to the bacteriological discoveries of Louis Pasteur. Suddenly the language needed a word to convey the state of an animal or person protected from disease by inoculation, and 'immunity' fit the bill. It is with reference to Pasteur's prevention of anthrax in sheep, in fact, that we first find the word 'immune' used in this sense in English, in 1881. As is common with new meanings of old words, someone felt they had to criticize the use; our second quotation, from 1888, reads: 'But (to use the new medical barbarism) we are never "immune" altogether from the contagion.' Presumably people were just too happy to be immune from nasty diseases to continue fretting about whether the word was a 'barbarism'! 'Immunize' dates from 1892, when it was first used in translating a German text.

INOCULATION

The Latin word *oculus* meant 'eye' and has of course given us words like 'ocular' and 'binocular'. But it also meant a bud on a plant, and *inoculare* meant to graft a bud of one plant onto another. This came into English as 'inoculate' in the 1400s. For the next 300 years, 'inoculation' referred only to plants. Then in the early 1700s people started experimenting with injecting people with the smallpox virus in order to bring on a mild attack of the disease. This practice started in the East, and spread to western Europe through Constantinople. Because of the similarity between grafting a foreign plant onto another plant, and the idea of introducing foreign matter into the body, the word 'inoculation' was used for this new procedure. Then in 1796, Edward Jenner discovered that you could achieve the same immunity with less danger by using the cowpox virus. And it is to Jenner that we owe not only humanity's liberation from the scourge of smallpox, but also the word 'vaccine'.

VACCINE
Being an 18th-century guy, Jenner had to give a Latin name to the disease known to Gloucestershire dairy farmers as 'cowpox', so he called it *variolae vaccinae*, from the Latin for cow, *vacca*. He used this Latin form as an adjective to create new English words: 'vaccine disease' (cowpox) and 'vaccine inoculation' for the injection with cowpox virus. Only a year after Jenner published his discoveries, the unwieldy 'vaccine inoculation' was already being rivalled by 'vaccination'. And it was Pasteur, in 1881, who started to use the word 'vaccination' for inoculation against any disease, not just smallpox.

PHARMACY
Pharmakon was the Greek word for 'drug', but it was also their word for 'poison'. A pharmacist friend of mine says quite matter-of-factly that this makes perfect sense, because if you take enough of anything it will kill you!

AMBULANCE
'Ambulance' comes from Latin *ambulare*, meaning 'to walk'. In the 1500s, the French (possibly Rabelais, who loved using Latinate words) had created the word *ambulant* to mean 'travelling, itinerant'. A French medical invention dating from 1762 was the *hôpital ambulant*, a mobile hospital that followed armies around. By 1792, this had been shortened to *ambulance*, a term which the English borrowed to describe the ones they saw the French using during the Napoleonic wars. 'Ambulance' also

came to apply to a wagon or cart that was part of one of these early 19th-century MASH units. During the Crimean War, when the French were allies, the English adopted this extended use as well. Eventually the word came to apply to any vehicle used to transport the sick or injured.

Be Mine

&

Valentine's Day, and love is in the air. Love is also in the dictionary, with definitions like the following, from the *Oxford English Dictionary*:

> That disposition or state of feeling with regard to a person which (arising from recognition of attractive qualities, from instincts of natural relationship, or from sympathy) manifests itself in solicitude for the welfare of the object, and usually also in delight in his or her presence and desire for his or her approval.

This kind of takes the romance out of it, and probably explains why lexicographers don't top people's lists as the dream date for a romantic evening! If only they knew what fascinating stories we could tell them about words relating to love…

ROMANCE
'Romance' started out as a French word, *romanz*, meaning the vernacular language of France, what we would call Old French. This was opposed to classical Latin on the one hand, and Frankish on the other hand. The linguistic situation in France (or

Gaul) after the fall of the Roman Empire was that most of the people were speaking this derivative of Latin, and then it was invaded by the Franks. So they had to distinguish between these two vernaculars. The corruption of Latin that most of the people spoke was called the 'Roman manner', and that's why it ended up being *romanz*.

By extension, the word came to apply to any written narrative in Old French. This explains why the modern French word for 'novel' is *roman*. One of the most popular genres back in medieval France was a narrative recounting the adventures of some hero of chivalry, and this became known as the 'courtly romance'. A very significant theme in these was courtly love, or the devoted idealized service of the knight to his lady (like Lancelot and Guinevere or Tristan and Isolde). The man was absolutely devoted to the service of his lady, no matter how capricious her whims. Now, this was a literary notion, and it was a concept of love that had not existed in western civilization before. It spread like wildfire throughout European literature and actually became part of everyone's mindset. Since the stories in which this love was exemplified were called 'romances', the word 'romance' itself became synonymous with that kind of love. I think most of us think that the way we engage in romantic love is just innate human behaviour, but in fact we owe a lot of it to a literary conceit originating in medieval Provence. It's interesting to note, when looking at the influence of the courtly romance, that although the word 'love' itself dates back to Anglo-Saxon times, the phrases 'be in love' and 'fall in love' cropped up in English only in the 1400s, when they were translated from French. I really don't know how they conveyed this idea before then.

PASSION

It will come as no surprise to anyone suffering from unrequited love (which of course we hope is not the case for any of our readers) that 'passion' originally meant 'suffering'. This was the sense of Latin *passionem*, and it still survives in the name of the parts of the Gospels that recount the suffering and death of Jesus, the St Matthew Passion and so on. For a while in the Middle Ages, 'passion' could even mean 'pain', so you could say, 'I have a passion in my foot', meaning 'my foot hurts'.

Because of the sense of suffering, 'passion' could also mean any strong emotion that afflicted you. Since love is a very strong emotion, the word gradually got applied to love, and particularly to sexual love. But if you are planning on serving your sweetheart passionfruit on Valentine's Day as being particularly appropriate, I'm sorry to have to tell you that you've got the wrong passion. Passionfruit is so called because it is the fruit of the passionflower, which got its name because the parts of the flower recall the Crucifixion: the blossom looks like the crown of thorns, the stamens represent Christ's five wounds, and the styles look like nails.

TERMS OF ENDEARMENT

It is surprising how old some terms of endearment are. We have evidence of 'darling' from Alfred the Great in about 800, of 'my love' from 1225, of 'sweetheart' from 1290, and of 'honey' from 1350. Unfortunately, words like 'snookums' and 'sweetie-pie' were not in King Alfred's vocab; they date only from the early 20th century.

BOUQUET

'Bouquet' started out in French as a word meaning a grove of trees (that would be an interesting thing to send your lover on Valentine's Day). It was a diminutive of a Germanic word *bosk*, from which the English word 'bush' also ultimately comes. So a *bouquet* was a clump of trees, but the French started to say, redundantly, '*un bouquet d'arbres*', which technically meant 'a clump of trees of trees'. It must be said that we have the same redundancy in English when we say 'a grove of trees' because you can't have a grove of anything else. So, the French, with *'bouquet d'arbres'* began to think that *bouquet* meant 'clump' or 'bunch' in relation to plants, so they started talking about a *'bouquet de fleurs'* or a bunch of flowers. We borrowed *bouquet* from them, only in the flower sense, in the early 1700s, when it was terribly trendy for the English to show off that they had been to France. It was a time when young men went on the Grand Tour of Europe (ostensibly to broaden their education but also to engage in some dissipation at a safe distance from home) and brought back a lot of French words to England.

PHILANDER

A florist I know once told me that the men calling up on Valentine's Day to order bouquets often want one for their wife and one for their mistress, so perhaps this is also a good time to look at the word 'philander'. It was originally a noun, coming from two Greek words: *philo* meaning 'loving' and *andros* meaning 'man'. So in Greek this meant a lover of men! It was also applied to women, however, and meant a woman who loved her husband. In the Renaissance, several European languages picked up this Greek word but were confused by its meaning, thinking it meant 'a loving man; a male lover', and it was used as the proper name for the stereotypical young lover in many plays and poems. This proper name, Philander, was quite common in literature in the late 1600s, and by the early 1700s we had turned it into the verb that we now know, meaning, as the OED puts it in its inimitable fashion, 'to make love, especially in a trifling manner; to flirt; to dangle after a woman'. 'Philanderer' didn't crop up for another hundred years, in the mid-1800s.

WITH EASTER FAST
APPROACHING

છ

Sometime in February you're almost certain to find Ash Wednesday, or the beginning of Lent (which incidentally comes immediately after the Sunday known as 'Quinquagesima'—my favourite word). So this is a good time to turn our attention to things Lenten other than the difficulty of surviving without chocolate for six weeks.

LENT

Lent is the forty-day liturgical season of penance and abstinence leading up to Easter, and indeed its French name, *Carême*, is a squishing-down of the Latin *Quadragesima*, which means 'fortieth'. The residents of Gaul were very good at dropping extraneous consonants and syllables out of words as they passed from Latin to Old French, and, faced with words like *Quadragesima*, who can blame them? But if the French word for this season is of Latinate origin, as one would expect with churchy things, why isn't the English one?

'Lent' is actually a shortened form of the Anglo-Saxon word for 'spring', *Lenten*. It may be related to the word 'length', referring to the progressive lengthening of the days at this time of year. Most years, Canadians would find it laughable to associate the beginning of Lent with spring, but you can just see it making sense in the south of England. The Church was very canny about adopting Old English words for its purposes, so, just as they did with 'Easter', they took an already existing word and applied it to an ecclesiastical reality, to make it more palatable to the newly converted. I'm sure associating the time before Easter with the pleas-

ures of spring was a much better marketing ploy for luring con-
verts than choosing a word that emphasized the forty long days of
fasting and all-round mortification!

HALIBUT

Speaking of fasting brings us to the practice of eating fish during
Lent and on other holy days and in particular to the word 'halibut'.
'Butt' was used for various kinds of flatfish in the Middle Ages,
possibly because their heads had a blunt shape like the butt-end
of something. As we saw at Christmas, 'hally' (also pronounced
'holly') was how the word we know as 'holy' was pronounced in
the Middle Ages. A 'hally butt' was, therefore, a flatfish eaten on
holy days, a 'holy flatfish'. Alas, it is not recorded whether a
medieval Robin went around saying 'Halibut, Batman!'

SOLE

The sole is another flatfish, and it is so called because it looks like
the sole of a shoe. This word comes from the Latin *solea,* which
meant 'sandal'. 'Sole' in the sense of 'only' comes from another
Latin word, *solus*, meaning 'alone', which has given us the word
'solitude'. But both the fish and the bottom of your shoe are from
the same root originally.

LEMON SOLE

Many people probably think that lemon sole is sort of like lemon
chicken: it's just sole prepared with lemons. But the word 'lemon'
has nothing to do with the fruit in this case. It's a corruption of
the French word *limande*, which was applied to a number of flatfish. *Limande* comes in turn from a Gaulish word which meant
'plank' (again, all of these fish are very flat). Indeed, there is a very
entertaining idiom in European French, '*elle est plate comme une
limande*', the equivalent of 'she is flat as a board'. The other lemon,
the fruit, came to us via French from an Arabic word, *limun*,

which they used for any kind of citrus fruit. So absolutely no relation between the two lemons here.

ALBACORE
'Albacore' is a lovely word. The albacore is a very large type of tuna, and the word comes from two Arabic words, the Arabic definite article *al*, plus *bukr,* which meant 'young camel'. Nothing to do with fish originally. This Arabic word migrated into Portuguese as *bacoro*, and in Portuguese it didn't mean a camel (there not being too many of those in Portugal); it meant 'young pig', but still no connection to fish. But it's probably because the tuna in question is so huge and very tubby-shaped, not like the flatfish we were just talking about, that it got its name from a word meaning 'pig' or 'camel'. English borrowed it from Portuguese in the 1500s.

SKIPJACK
'Skipjack' is also the name of a kind of tuna. Various kinds of fish which have the habit of leaping (or 'skipping') out of the water have been called 'skipjack'. The word was first applied to fish around 1700, though it had been around since the 1500s, meaning, in the OED's inimitable definition, 'a pert shallow-brained fellow; a whipper-snapper; a conceited fop or dandy'.

THE ENVELOPE, PLEASE

%

February also brings the Academy Awards. And while we're talking about awards, we'll squeeze in the Canadian Junos, which usually happen a little later.

AWARD

The verb 'award' comes from an Old Norman French word meaning 'to look at; to consider'; surprisingly, it is the same word that has given us 'regard'. When the Norsemen invaded France, they brought the word *ewarder* with them. The central-French people couldn't pronounce *w*'s, so they stuck a *g* in it to make it easier to say—*eguarder*—and this eventually migrated into English several centuries later as 'regard'. Meanwhile, however, the Normans had set off to England taking their word forms with them. The English, being Germanic, had no problems with the *w* sound. The Normans imposed their legal system on the English, and 'award' first shows up in the legal sense of a judicial decision, that is, something arrived at after looking at a case and considering its merits. It wasn't until the 19th century that 'award' came to mean a prize in a contest. Funnily enough, our first evidence is from a magazine called *Poultry Chronicle,* stating that no award was given because none of the chickens was up to snuff!

ACADEMY

The original Academy was a garden near Athens where Plato taught. It was named after a legendary Greek hero called Akademos, and the spot was sacred to him. In the Renaissance, all things from ancient Greece were very trendy, so people adapted the name of Plato's school for their own educational institutions. By the late 17th century, the name came to be used of societies whose goal was the furtherance of some art or science.

OSCAR

The story goes that a former secretary at the Academy of Motion Picture Arts and Sciences is said to have remarked in 1931 that the statuette (first awarded in 1928) reminded her of her 'Uncle Oscar'—Oscar Pierce, a farmer. The name stuck.

GRIP

On movie and TV credits you often see the titles 'key grip' and 'dolly grip'. 'Grip' is the term for a stagehand or technician on a film crew. This is an extension of a 19th-century American use of the word 'grip' to mean a stagehand, presumably because the stagehands had to have a good 'grip' on the sets, props, flywires, and so on. So the 'key grip' is the person in charge of all the stage-hands ('key' here being in the adjectival sense of 'most important'). The 'dolly grip' is the person who pushes or drives the dolly on which the camera operator moves around with the camera.

GAFFER

The gaffer is the head electrician on a film or television set. This is a 20th-century extension of a 19th-century use of the word to mean the foreman of a gang of workmen. The term dates back to Shakespeare's time as a term of respect for an elderly man, and is probably a contraction of 'godfather'.

JUNO

The Junos are the awards presented by the Canadian Academy of Recording Arts and Sciences for excellence in Canadian music recording—the Canadian Grammys. They were named punningly in 1971 for the Roman goddess and for Pierre Juneau, who, as chairman of the CRTC, introduced Canadian content rules for broadcasting.

LOTS OF HEBREW WORDS

℘

The Jewish festival of Purim falls sometime in March, providing an opportunity to look at words derived from Hebrew.

PURIM

Purim is a festival that celebrates the deliverance of the Jews from a planned extermination in the Persian empire in the 5th century BC. The story is recounted in the Book of Esther. The Persian king's prime minister, Haman, became enraged at the Jews when one of them, Mordecai, refused to bow down before him. So Haman convinced the king that all the Jews in his empire should be eliminated. But the king had a Jewish wife—this was Esther—who interceded with him at the risk of her own life to spare the Jews. The king granted her request and had Haman hanged. The day on which the slaughter of the Jews was to take place had been selected by Haman by drawing lots, and *purim* is the Hebrew word for 'lots'. Since it turned out to be a day when the Jews defeated their enemies instead and emerged triumphant, Purim is quite a joyous festival.

HAMANTASCHEN

It's traditional on Purim to eat a kind of triangular cookie with a prune or poppyseed filling. These are supposed to look like Haman's three-cornered hat, and thus the cookies are called 'hamantaschen' or 'Haman's hat'.

JUBILEE

'Jubilee' is a word that, surprisingly, comes from an ancient Hebrew word meaning 'ram'. That's the male sheep kind of ram, not the computer RAM, the latter being rather scarce amongst the ancient Hebrews. The word was *yobel*, and it came to apply not only to the rams themselves but also to the rams' horns used for making trumpets that were blown on religious occasions.

According to a religious custom described in Leviticus, every fifty years the ancient Jews observed a year during which slaves were freed and people who had been forced to mortgage their land had it returned to them. It's uncertain whether these years were ever in fact observed, or whether it was just laid down in Leviticus; but they were described as being initiated by the blowing of the ram's horn trumpet on Yom Kippur. And so the name of the trumpet came also to apply to the year.

The Romans got hold of *yobel* when they were translating the Bible into Latin, but they confused it with a word used by Roman country folk, *jubilare*, which essentially meant 'yell out to attract attention' (and which of course gave us 'jubilation'). So *yobel* became *jubilaeus* and ended up in English as 'jubilee'. Originally the word 'jubilee' was used only in reference to this Hebrew custom in the Bible, but then the Catholic Church invented its own kind of jubilee to be celebrated every fifty years (now every twenty-five years) to be observed as a special time of penitence, almsgiving, and pilgrimage. Eventually the idea of a special anniversary became attached to the word, and that's why we use 'jubilee' as we do today. No rams need apply.

SHIBBOLETH

Shibboleth is one of my favourite words! A shibboleth is something—a custom, practice, belief, or way of speaking—that identifies you as belonging to one group rather than another. So the way we Canadians pronounce 'out' and the fact that we call sofas 'chesterfields' are shibboleths of Canadian English. The story behind 'shibboleth' is recounted in the Bible, in Judges, and it's quite cute. *Shibboleth* was the Hebrew word for an ear of wheat, or possibly meant 'flood water'. At one point, two of the tribes of Israel, the Ephraimites and the Gileadites, were at war. The Gileadites used the word 'shibboleth' as a password. The Ephraimites couldn't say it; they said 'sibboleth' instead. The English reading the Bible learned this particular lesson rather too well, so that in 1658 we come across this quotation: 'They had a Shibboleth to discover them, he who pronounced *Brot* and *Cawse* for *Bread* and *Cheese* had his head lopt off.'

BEHEMOTH

Behemoth was the name of a creature mentioned in the book of Job. It is the plural of the word for 'beast' in Hebrew and therefore could be interpreted as a particularly beastly kind of beast, because the plural was often used in Hebrew as a kind of intensifier. 'Behemoth' could also be an assimilation to Hebrew of an Egyptian word meaning 'water ox', which could have designated either the hippopotamus or the crocodile—both creatures that the Jews would have encountered only in Egypt. It has been used figuratively to mean 'a very large thing' since the late 1500s.

MAVEN

This comes to us via Yiddish from a Hebrew word *mebin,* which meant a person with understanding, a teacher. Nowadays, we use it mostly to mean 'expert', but originally it seems to have had more of the connotations of 'connoisseur' or 'fancier'. We owe its popularity in English to an advertising campaign for a brand of herring in 1964. The slogans were 'tell them the herring maven sent you' or 'The herring maven has struck again', with a picture of an empty jar of herring.

RRSP Season

March 1 is the deadline to make your RRSP contribution for the previous tax year. As you rush madly to the bank, you may stop and look at the rates being offered for GICs . Both 'RRSP' and 'GIC' are, by the way, Canadianisms, but you probably don't spend much time reflecting on that as you stand aghast at the paltry interest rates. But you may have wondered how the word 'interest' came to be attached to financial transactions, and about other words related to pensions.

PENSION
'Pension' comes from a Latin word *pensus* meaning 'weighed'. Back in Roman times, the way they paid people was to weigh the gold or silver, so *pensus* came to mean a payment. Originally in English in the 1400s, a pension was any kind of payment or wage, but it soon came to apply to a payment made to people after they had retired.

FUND
Fund comes from the Latin *fundus* meaning 'the bottom', which of course has also given us 'fundamental'. But *fundus* could also mean a plot of land, especially one which was someone's property. Then as now, land was a source of wealth, so people started using 'fund' to mean a permanent supply of money that could be drawn on, just as you could draw on your 'fund' of land for food and so on.

INVEST
'Invest' and 'vestment' are related, surprisingly enough. They both come ultimately from the Latin word *vestis,* meaning clothing. *Investire* in Latin meant 'to clothe'. It takes a little bit of thinking to figure out how on earth clothing came to be connected with putting your money in something. It was the Italians who were to blame, and not necessarily because of their reputation for being snappy dressers. In medieval Italian, in about the 1300s, *investire* took on another meaning. This was about the time when Italy started to be very wealthy, and banks arose as an institution. There was a lot of economic activity going on that people could provide money for. The idea was that, if you took your money and used it to buy a textile mill or to finance Marco Polo's trips east to bring back spices, it was as if you were putting a new suit of clothes on

your money. You were transforming it into something else—hopefully, more money in the long run! This usage came into English in the 1600s through the East India Company, which probably encountered it by contact with the Spanish and the Portuguese who were looking for spices in the East Indies at the same time as the English.

INTEREST

In Latin, *interest* means 'it's important'. In Old French this became *interet*, which meant a kind of damages that you pay to someone in compensation, obviously something that to the aggrieved party is very important indeed. Now, in the Middle Ages it was forbidden to charge money for lending money, since that was considered to be usury, which was a sin. But they had a crafty way of getting around this. Roman law had established the principle that, if someone defaulted on a loan, they had to pay an extra amount to the lender as compensation; this they called *interesse*. Then someone (a lender, no doubt) realized that the lender was penalized even if the debtor did repay the loan, because while the lender's money was in the debtor's hands, the lender was losing profit that he could otherwise have made. So lenders started writing into their loans an amount for 'damages', which they called 'interest', since 'interest' had this sense of compensatory damages. Originally, this was calculated as a fixed sum, but by the 1200s they were calculating it as a percentage of the loan paid at intervals.

This practice of charging interest was finally sanctioned by law under Henry VIII, but the theory was that it was still 'damages'. This just goes to show, I think, that the time-honoured commercial practice of using euphemisms was alive and well in the Middle Ages. Just as nowadays if you phone to order a ballet ticket you may get charged what the box office calls a 'convenience fee' (indeed I am sure it is convenient for them!), if your medieval loan shark called it 'interest' instead of, say, a 'usury charge', people wouldn't notice, would they? We would probably all be in favour of calling it 'interest' when we are being paid it and a 'usury charge' when we are being charged it!

RETIRE

The story of 'retire' is extraordinarily complicated. Anyone who knows French will immediately recognize the French word *retirer*, meaning 'withdraw', and this is indeed where 'retire' came from into English in the 1500s. Originally you would retire somewhere just to get away from the world, but by the mid-1600s it also meant giving up one's job.

The fascinating thing is where the French got *retirer* and its root *tirer*, which means 'pull'. It seems that *tirer* was shortened from *martirier*, which was the Old French word for the verb 'martyr'. 'Martyr' actually comes from a Greek word meaning 'witness', because a martyr was someone who bore witness to their faith in God. But the Old French speakers didn't know that. They thought *martirier*, or more precisely the form *martiriant*, which meant 'martyring', was made up of two parts: *mar* which meant 'misfortune', and *tirant*, a variant of 'tyrant', which meant 'executioner'. A fairly common medieval form of torture and execution was putting someone on a rack and pulling on their limbs so that they were dislocated. So people started to think that the *tirer* part of *martirier* meant 'pull'. And that's how *tirer* ended up as the French word for 'pull', ultimately producing the French word *retirer* and our word 'retire'.

INDEX 1: WORDS

fear, xv
feckless, 186
fedora, 21
feign, 192
fellow, 2
fiction, 192
fiddle, 116
figgy pudding, 164
figment, 192
finance, 32
fiscal, 32
flea market, 42
flu, 190
focus, 74
foolscap, 96
fork, 39
forsooth, 181
fouetté, 109
fuel, 74
fund, 208
fundamental, 208
futon, xiv
gaffer, 204
gage, 27
gallop, 6
galoshes, 168
gamble, 187
game, 187
garage, 41
garden, 38
gas, 73
gasoline, 74
geek, 94
genteel, 162
ginger, 161
gingerbread, 161
gingerly, 162
glamour, 92
go, 104
golf, 86
govern, ix

gown, 53
grade, 47
gradual, 46
gradual psalm, 46
graduate, xiii, 46
graduation, 46
grammar, 92
grape, 69
grapple, 69
grass, 39
greyhound, 65
grip, 204
grog, 173
groggy, 174
grogram, 173
groom, 53
ground truth, 139
gruel, 99
gruelling, 99
gruesome, 185
guarantee, xii
guardian, xii
gumboots, 170
gumshoe, 170
gym, 128
gymnasium, 128
gymnastic, 128
gymnastics, 128
hack, 14
hackney, 14
halcyon days, 25
hale, 155
halibut, 201
Halliday, 154
hamantaschen, 205
hamper, 58
hat, 20
hay fever, 41
hazard, 86
hearse, 84
hearty, 155

heaven, 81
hectic, 150
hedge, 39
herb, 120
highway, 73
hippodrome, 191
hoarfrost, 170
hoary, 66
hobnob, 177
hoe, 39
holiday, 154
holy, 154, 201
honcho, 144
honey, 198
hooch, 172
hood, 20
hopscotch, 102
horehound, 66
hospice, 16
hospital, xi, 15
hostel, xi, 15
hotel, xi, 15
hound, 64
house, viii
huckster, 142
hurricane, 79
hypocrite, 110
idiot strings, 168
immune, 193
immunity, 193
immunize, 194
impact, xv
income tax, 27
infant, 178
infantry, 178
influence, 190
influenza, 190
inn, 16
inoculate, 194
inoculation, 194
instruct, 115

INDEX 2: LANGUAGES

∽

Abenaki
toboggan, 166

Anglo-Saxon
ant, 59
anthem, 17, 18
barrow, 39
beer, 173
bird, 119
bitch, 65
book, 96
bread, 30
breed, viii
bridal, 51
bride, 51
bridegroom, 51
calf, ix
Chapman, 43
cheap, 43
cheese, 131
clod, 81
cloud, 81
clover, 39
cottage, 36
cow, ix
crumb, 59
darling, 198
dig, 39
dog, 64
dovecote, 36
dung, 40
Easter, 17
eat, viii
'em, ix
England, viii

fare, 10
farewell, 10
fart, 25
fear, xv
fiddle, 116
fork, 39
gamble, 187
game, 187
garden, 38
grass, 39
greyhound, 65
groom, 52
halibut, 201
Halliday, 154
Halloween, 154
hedge, 39
highway, 73
hoarfrost, 66, 170
hoary, 66
hoe, 39
holiday, 154
holy, 154
horehound, 66
hound, 64
house, viii
inn, 16
Lent, 200
let, 78
loaf, 30
loom, 23
love, 197
man, viii
mark, 47
mow, 39
nickname, 157

overwhelm, 151
pea, 68
pease, 68
plant, 39
pool, 188
rake, 39
ride, 72
road, 72
root, 5
scot-free, 187
shack, 38
sheep, ix
short shrift, 148
shot, 187
shriek, ix, 186
shrub, 39
sneeze, 191
soothe, 181
spade, 39
spew, 192
steward, 12
Stewart, 11
sty, 12
swain, 5
swoon, 192
tree, 39
Wales, 159
walnut, 159
wassail, 155
way, 73
wed, 50
wedding, 50
wedlock, 51
weed, 39
weep, 180

French

abet, 188
adage, 107
admiral, 132
advise, ix
aisle, 55
ambulance, 195
apron, 61
award, 203
bank, 30
baroque, 19
beef, ix
beret, 21
bet, 187
bidet, 8
bilge, 32
blanket, 59
bonnet, 20
bordello, 83
bouquet, 198
bourrée, 109
boutique, 151
braise, ix
brochure, 142
buccaneer, 63
budget, 31
bulge, 32
bumf, 141
cab, 13
cabin, 37
cad, 88
caddy, 87
cadet, 88
camouflage, 134
candy, 158
carouse, 176
cash, 28
cattle, xi
chalet, 37
champion, 125
chattel, xi

cheat, 100
cheer, 175
cherry, 68
cider, 174
cloak, 139
coach, 127
coin, 143
colonel, 132
corsage, 53
court, ix
Courtauld, 7
cream, 122
cretin, 146
cry, 180
currant, 70
curtail, 7
dainty, 161
debt, 35
degree, 47
diaper, 179
dime, 28
dragoon, 133
entrechat, 107
entrepreneur, 144
essay, 97
exchequer, 34
faint, 192
farce, 112
fedora, 21
finance, 32
flea market, 42
fouetté, 109
fuel, 74
gage, 27
gallop, 6
galoshes, 169
garage, 41
ginger, 162
gingerbread, 161
gingerly, 162
govern, ix

gown, 53
grape, 69
grog, 174
groggy, 174
grogram, 174
gruel, 99
gruelling, 99
guarantee, xii
guardian, xii
hazard, 86
hearse, 84
herb, 120
hospice, 16
hostel, xi, 15
hotel, xi, 15
infant, 178
interest, 209
isle, 55
jelly, 67
journey, 10
journeyman, 10
junket, 58
lampoon, 176
lawn, 39
lemon, 201
lemon sole, 201
lieutenant, 131
limousine, 12
lozenge, 192
manoeuvre, 39
manure, 39
melon, 70
mince, 162
mincemeat, 162
mitten, 167
money, 143
mutton, ix
napkin, 62
orange, 157
pant, 126
parchment, 48